MANTEGNA
THE TRIUMPHS OF CAESAR

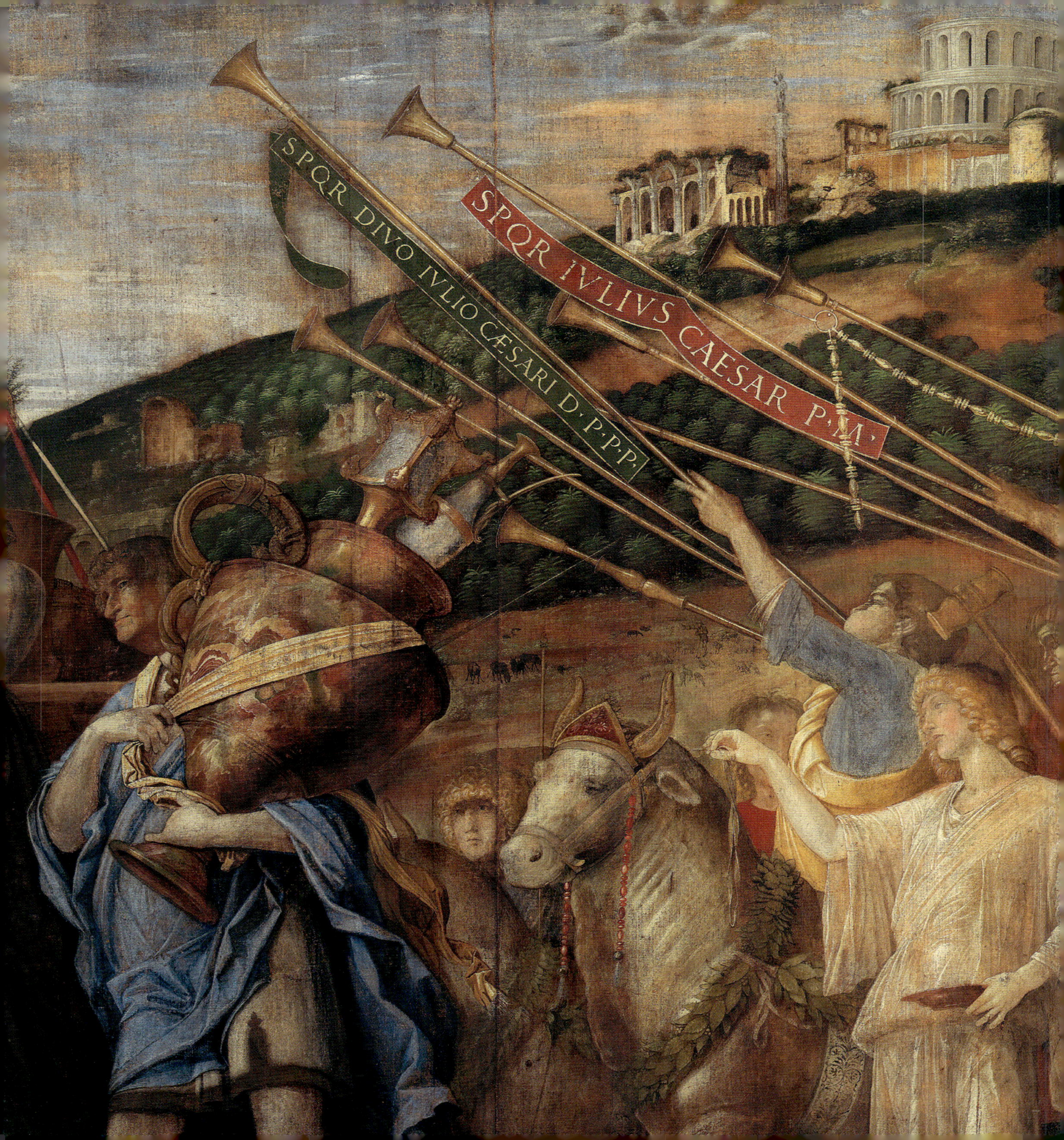
SPQR DIVO IVLIO CÆSARI D·P·P·P·
SPQR IVLIVS CAESAR P·M·

MANTEGNA
THE TRIUMPHS OF CAESAR

CAROLINE ELAM and GUIDO REBECCHINI

NATIONAL GALLERY GLOBAL, LONDON
DISTRIBUTED BY YALE UNIVERSITY PRESS

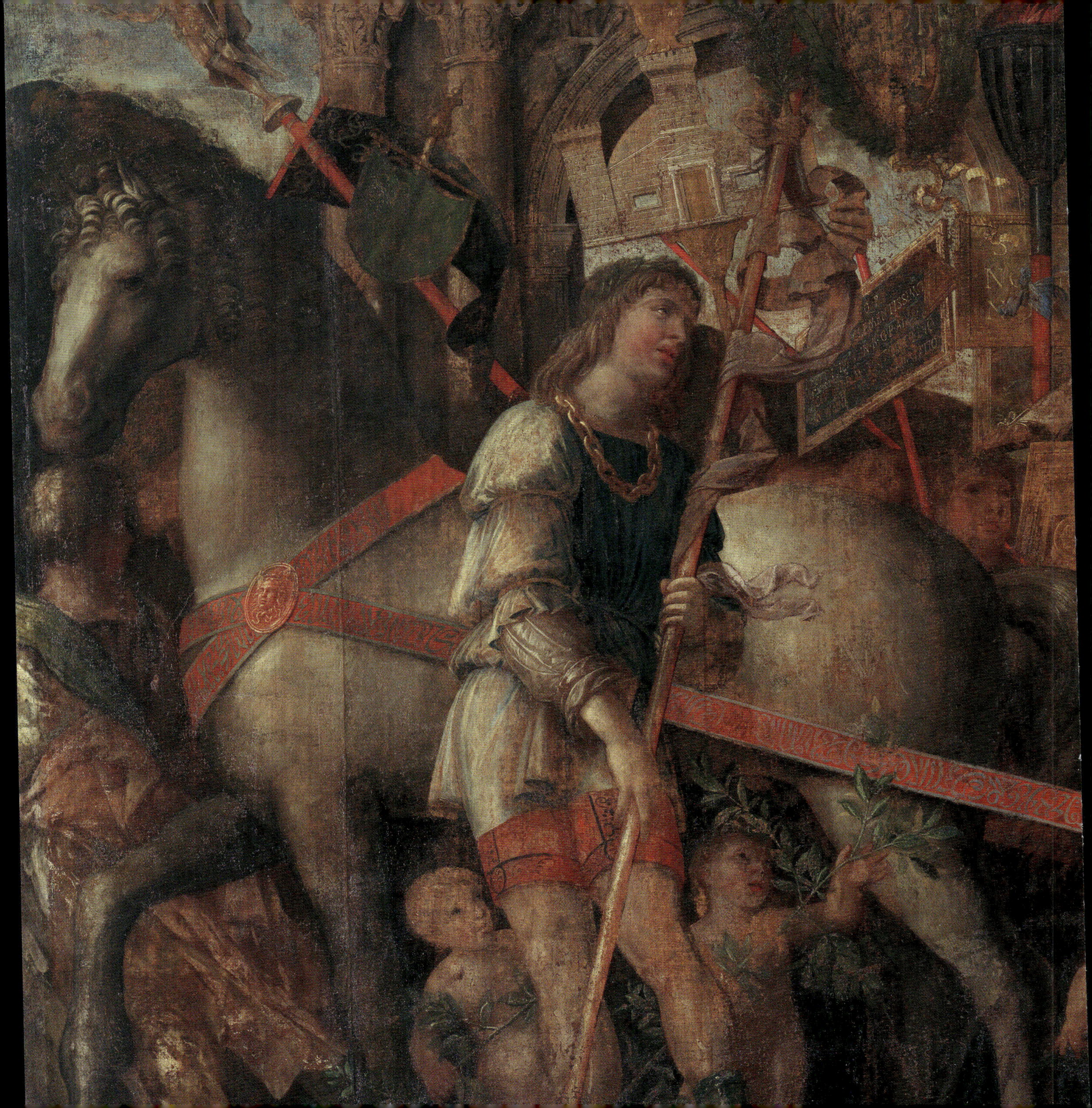

CONTENTS

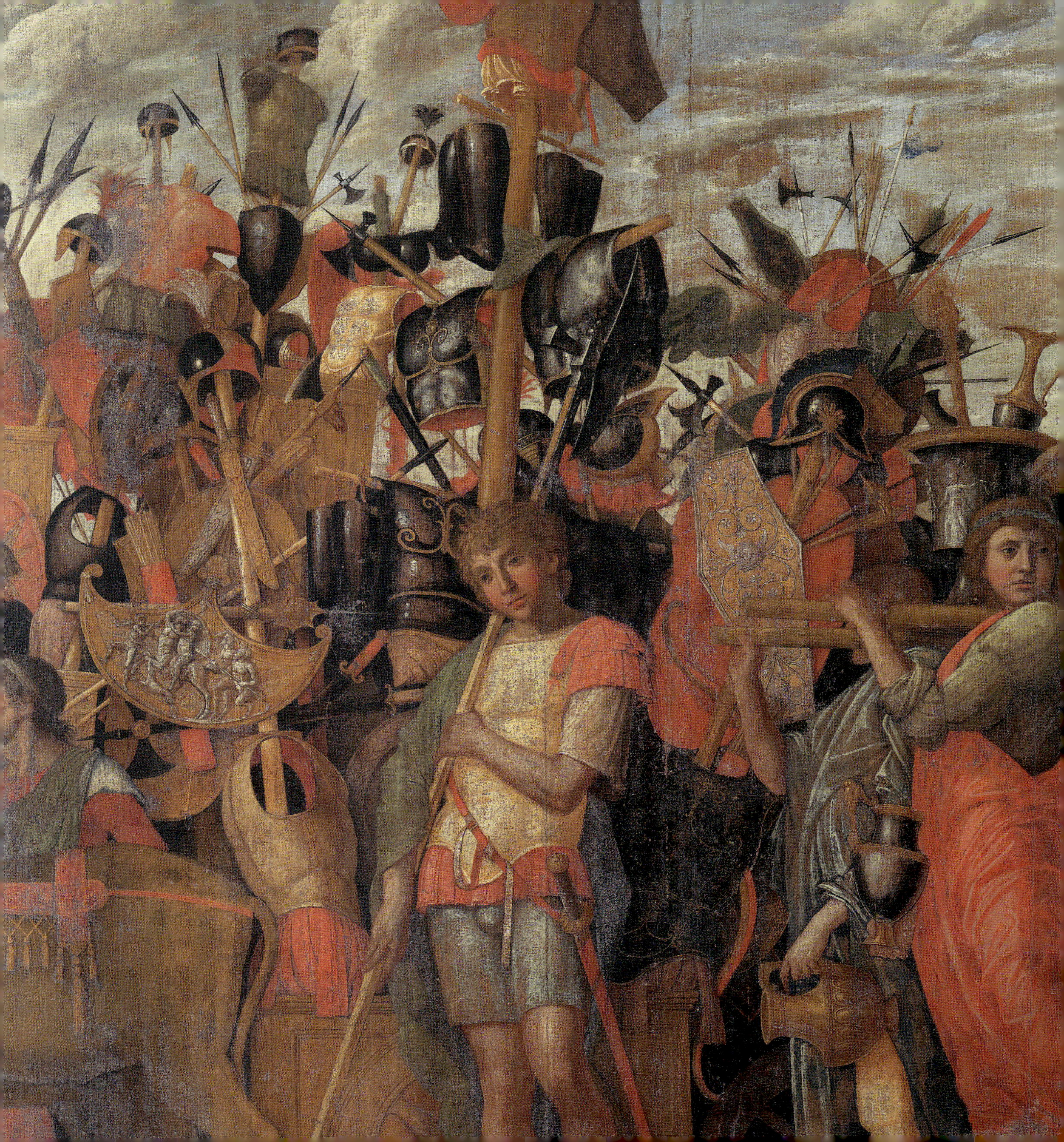

DIRECTOR'S FOREWORD

GABRIELE FINALDI

About 140 years after Andrea Mantegna painted *The Triumphs of Caesar*, the nine canvases were packed into boxes in Mantua for shipping to London where they arrived in 1630. They had been acquired from the ruling Gonzaga family to form part of the collection of the recently crowned Charles I of England, who was transforming his court into a glittering centre for the arts and whose deep interest in painting was already celebrated across Europe. Together with Raphael's cartoons of the *Acts of the Apostles*, which Charles had bought a few years earlier (they too remain in the Royal Collection and have been on loan since the nineteenth century to the Victoria & Albert Museum), they constitute the most important complete series of Italian Renaissance paintings outside of Italy.

Mantegna's canvases are a sustained, compelling and celebratory rendition of a Roman triumphal procession on a large scale. No other painter before him had sufficient familiarity with the subject to be able to realise such an all-embracing vision. He studied the visual sources – primarily ancient reliefs on triumphal arches and elsewhere – and read the relevant Latin texts in the library of the Gonzagas, and no doubt turned for further help to the scholars of classical antiquity he knew in Padua and Mantua. His rigorous analysis allied with his artistic imagination created impressive images of trumpeting soldiers, towering trophies of arms, bearers of gold bullion, oxen garlanded for sacrificial slaughter, long-trunked elephants, musicians and prisoners, and Caesar himself on a chariot crowned by a winged victory figure. The procession snakes and sways against a backdrop of viaducts and towers, hills, ruins and city buildings. It is accompanied by martial music, the clatter of arms, the bellowing and bleating of animals and the shouting of bystanders.

It seems very likely that the series was commissioned by Francesco II Gonzaga, although it remains a distinct possibility that the artist himself proposed the subject. Mantegna called them '*li trionfi mei*' and both court artist and patron knew that they would bring lustre to the reputation of both. The Gonzagas were *condottieri*, Renaissance warlords, and the association with Julius Caesar, the ancient victorious general *par excellence*, was highly desirable. In Mantegna's own lifetime, the *Triumphs* garnered the artist fame and by the middle of the sixteenth century they were considered by Vasari to be 'the best thing he had ever made'.

We are immensely grateful to His Majesty King Charles III, the National Gallery's Royal Patron, for lending six of the Mantegna canvases for our Bicentenary year 2024 and for the year of the reopening of the Gallery (2025) after major capital works, including a complete rehang of the national collection of paintings in Trafalgar Square. Normally on show at Hampton Court Palace under the care of Historic Royal Palaces, *The Triumphs of Caesar* are being seen in London by millions of people in the context of the largest and most representative collection of paintings by Mantegna anywhere in the world. We extend thanks also to Tim Knox, Director of the Royal Collection, and to Anna Reynolds, Surveyor of The King's Pictures. I am pleased to express my appreciation to the authors of this publication, distinguished art historian and friend Caroline Elam, and Guido Rebecchini, Professor at the Courtauld Institute of Art.

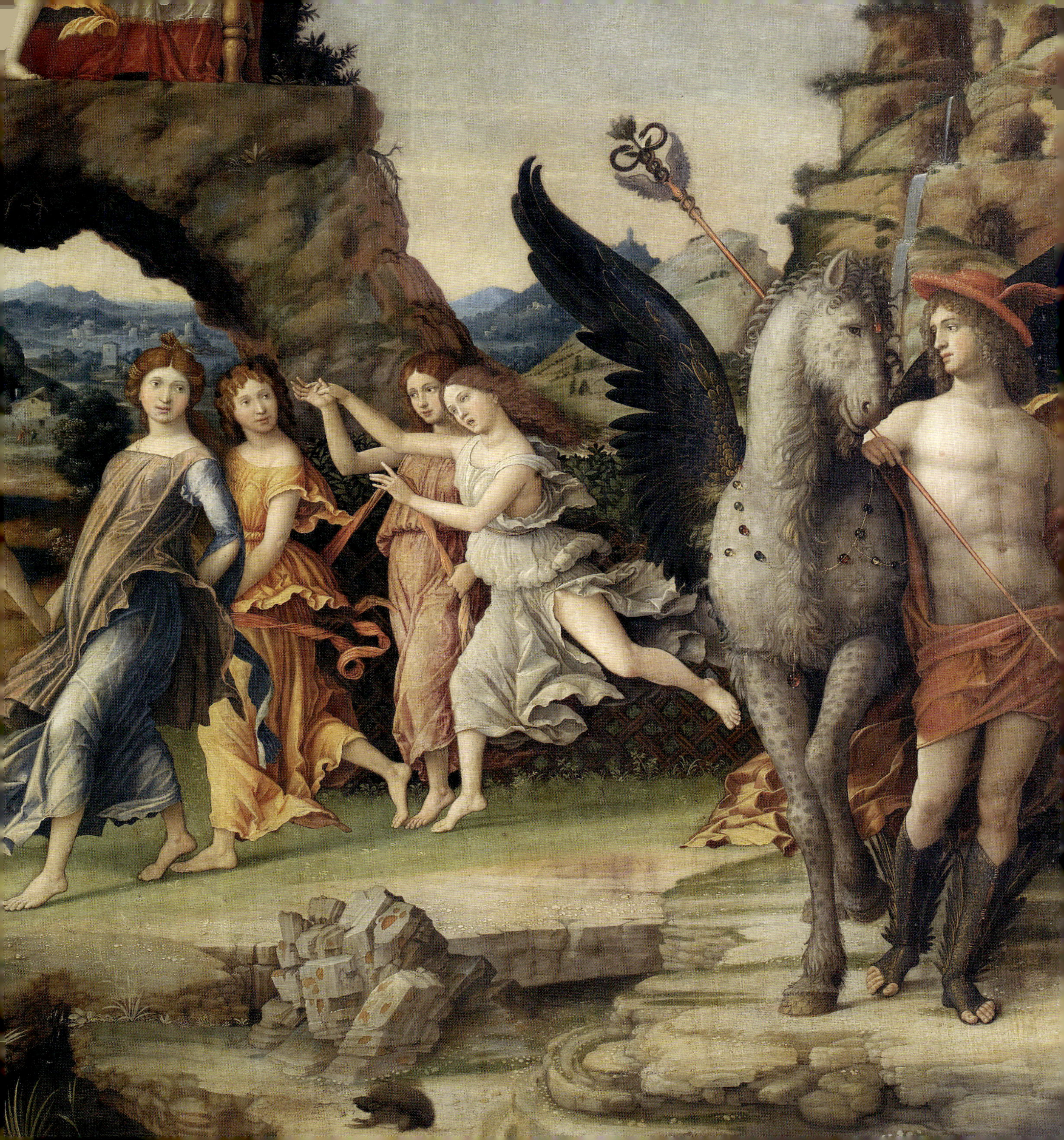

ANDREA MANTEGNA: COURT ARTIST TO THE GONZAGA OF MANTUA

GUIDO REBECCHINI

The arrival of Andrea Mantegna (1431–1506) at Mantua in 1460 revolutionised the course of the arts in the city. Trained in Padua in the workshop of Francesco Squarcione (1397–1468), where he had the opportunity to study ancient art and the sculpture of Donatello (1386–1466), Mantegna was invited by Marquis Ludovico Gonzaga (ruled 1444–78) to move to his court in 1457. He was offered a generous salary, a home for the family, and food and firewood for six people.[1] By then he was 27 years old, had been married to the daughter of the painter Jacopo Bellini (1396–1470), Nicolosia, for four years, and could boast the decoration of the Ovetari chapel in the Paduan church of the Eremitani (1448–57), where he had frescoed the stories of Saints James and Christopher. This highly innovative decorative cycle, almost entirely destroyed by Allied bombs in March 1944, had drawn the attention of the Mantuan court: in it, Mantegna had demonstrated full mastery of perspective, had shown his highly refined antiquarian knowledge, and had displayed unprecedented narrative skills – all ingredients considered essential to put Mantua at the forefront of modern art.[2]

Mantegna's inventive skills had also been on full display in a panel painted in Padua around 1455, *The Agony in the Garden* (fig. 1).[3] Presumably inspired by a drawing by his father-in-law, Jacopo Bellini, Mantegna depicted Christ in prayer on a craggy rock formation with three daringly foreshortened apostles fast asleep at its foot. Christ's intense meditation is about to be disrupted

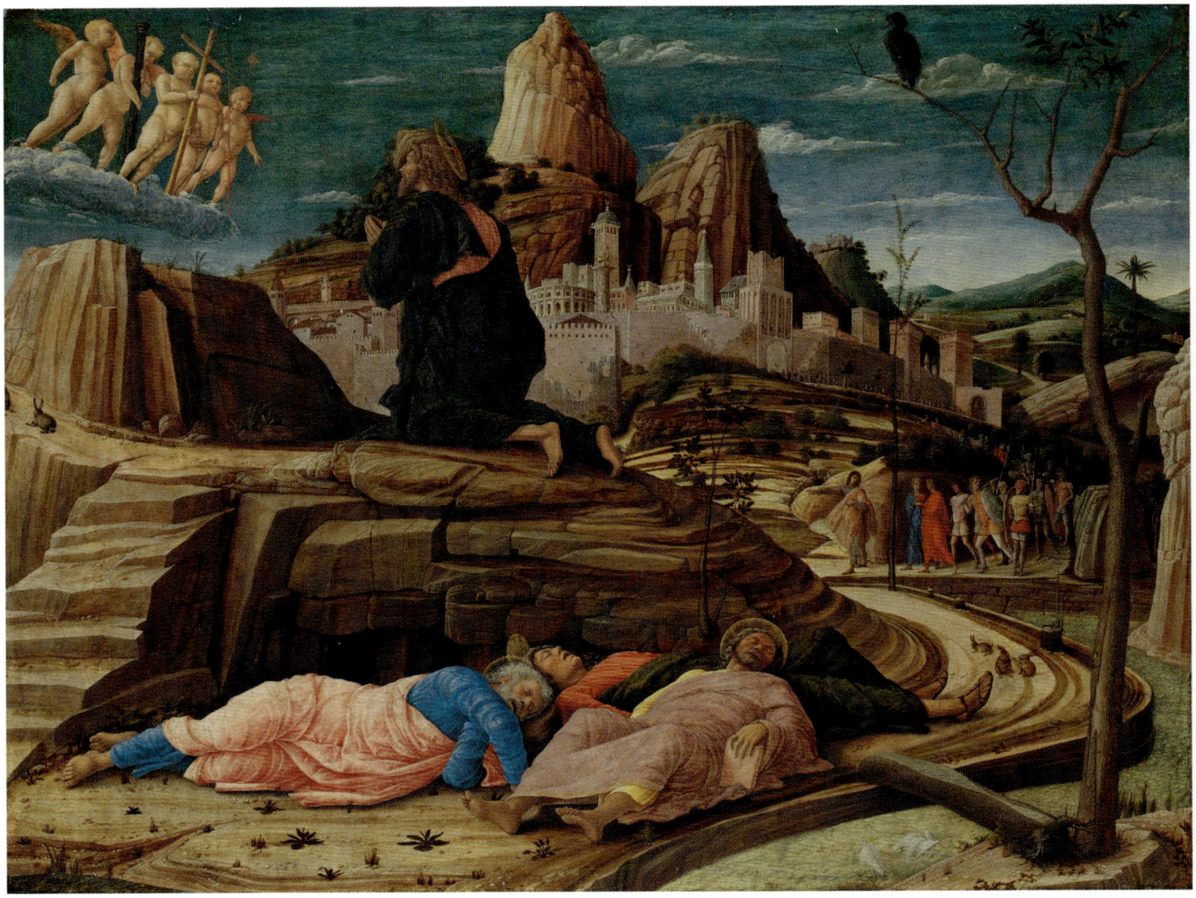

by the arrival of the Roman soldiers, creating a feeling of suspense and impending drama, heightened by a menacing bird of prey perched on a bare tree. In the background, Mantegna indulges in the minute description of an imaginary ancient city, which includes recognisable Roman landmarks such as the Colosseum and the Torre delle Milizie. This work stimulated Mantegna's brother-in-law, Giovanni Bellini (about 1435–1516), to engage in a pictorial dialogue by executing a painting of the same subject. Bellini's version – also in the National Gallery (around 1458–60) – although clearly inspired by Mantegna, remains distinctly different for its softer effects of natural light, revealing Bellini's unique sensitivity to atmospheric effects, in contrast with Mantegna's preference for crisp light and sharp contours.[4]

Mantegna's *Agony* anticipates the ambitious San Zeno altarpiece (fig. 2), which he painted for the main altar of the church of the same name in Verona. Its predella contained another meticulous depiction of *The Agony in the Garden*, now in the Musée des Beaux-Arts at Tours.[5] In this altarpiece, Mantegna displayed

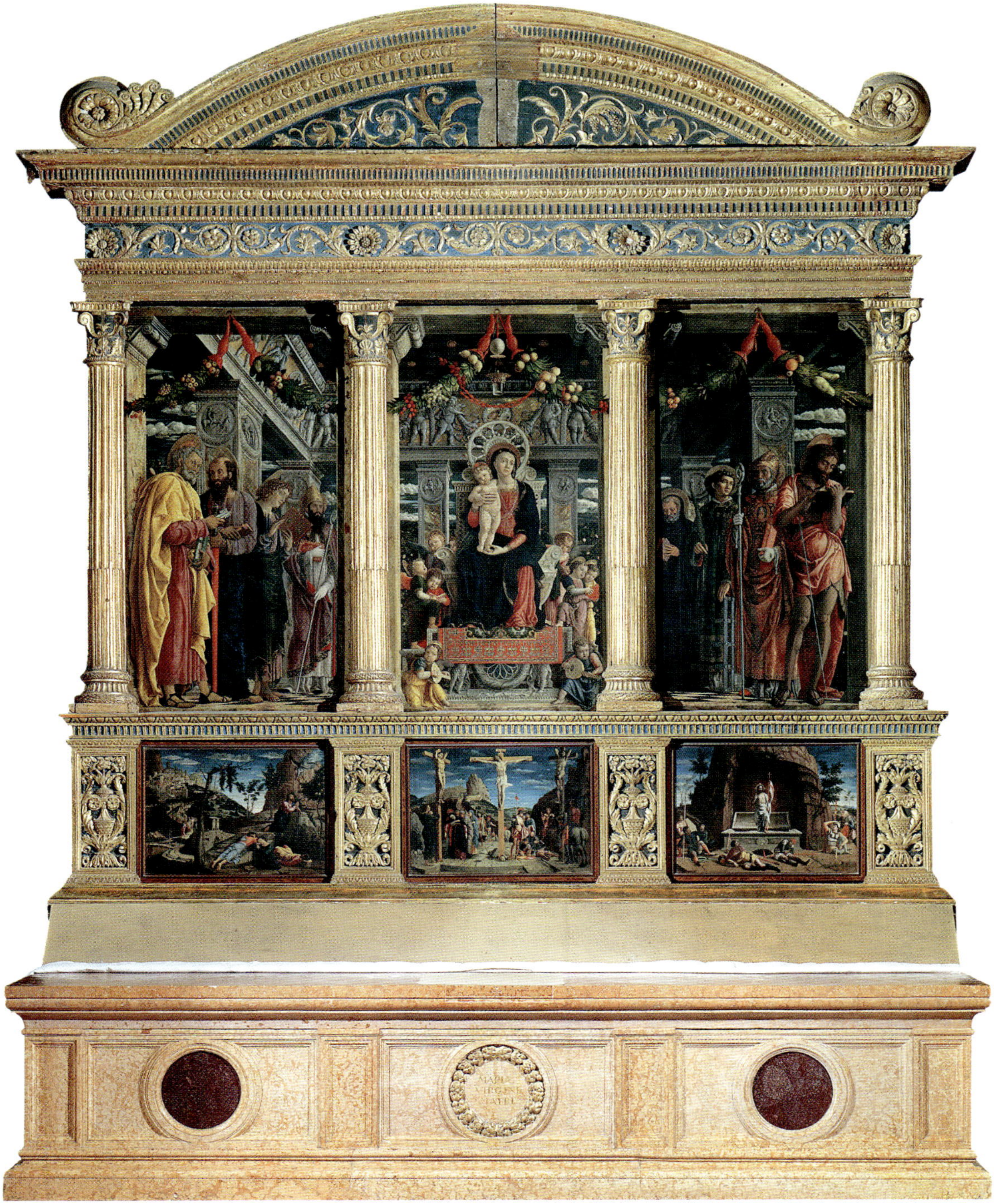

1 *The Agony in the Garden*, about 1455–6
Tempera on wood, 62.9 × 80 cm
The National Gallery, London

2 San Zeno altarpiece, about 1456–9
Tempera on poplar wood, 212 × 460 cm
Church of San Zeno, Verona

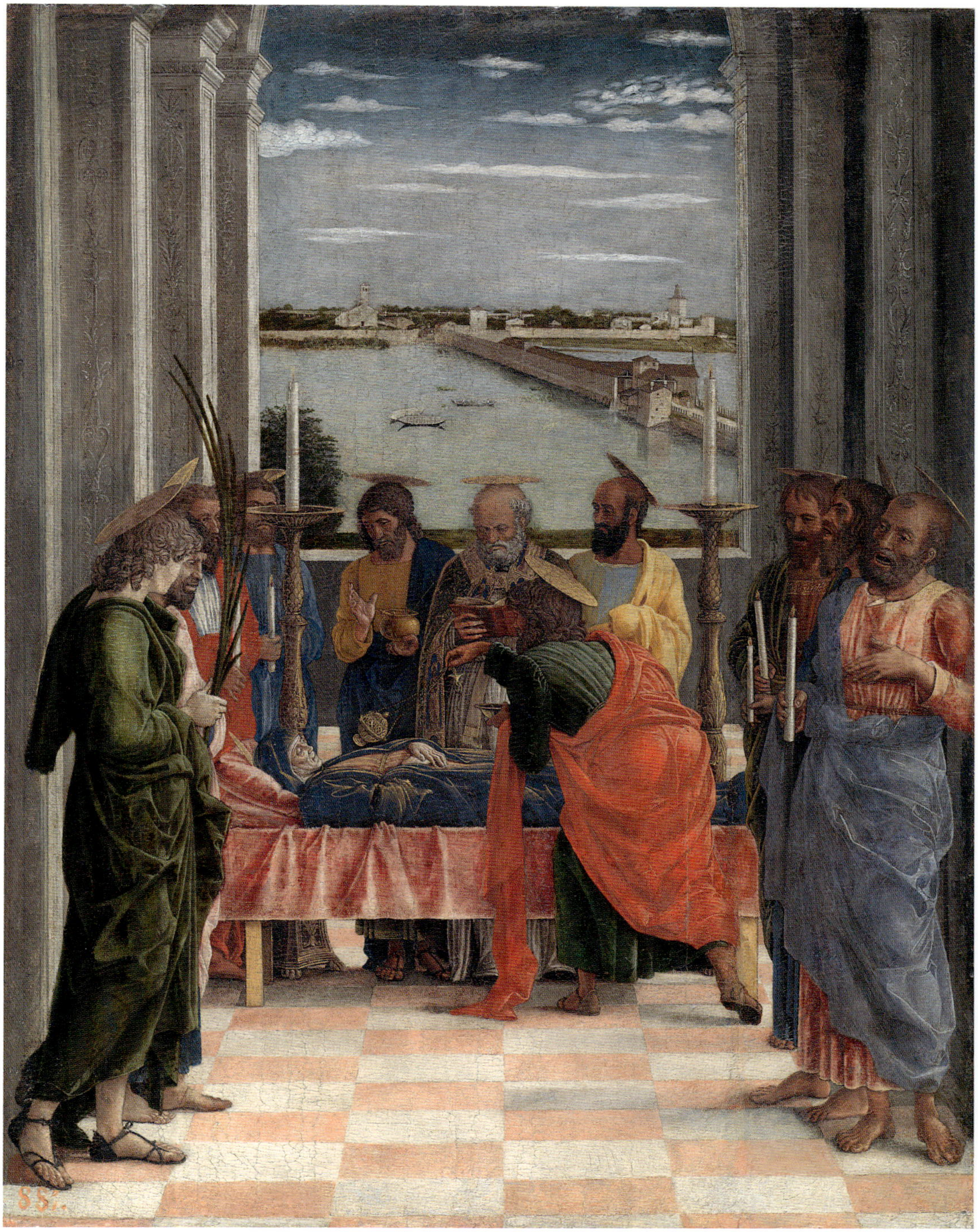

3 *The Death of the Virgin*, about 1462
Tempera and oil on wood, 54.5 × 42 cm
Museo Nacional del Prado, Madrid

a virtuoso combination of architectural illusionism and antiquarian references, which owed much to Donatello's bronze altar of the Santo in Padua (1446–53). The San Zeno altarpiece transformed the traditional polyptych format into a unified space in which the protagonists appear to move freely.[6] The extraordinary quality and innovative conception of this large and important work must have consolidated Ludovico Gonzaga's desire to bring the artist to Mantua, where Mantegna finally settled in 1460.

At work for the Gonzaga

By moving to Mantua, Mantegna accepted a position in the service of a lord, dependent on the latter's whims and self-aggrandising vision. What could have been perceived as a loss of freedom, however, turned out to be a gain, since Ludovico Gonzaga was a cultured prince who enthusiastically embraced the project of renewing his city's image: he had already secured as consultant the architect and humanist Leon Battista Alberti (1404–1472), who visited Mantua in 1459 while in the retinue of Pope Pius II (ruled 1458–64). During this visit, Mantua had revealed its inadequacy for the ambitions nurtured by the Gonzaga, and Mantegna's arrival shortly thereafter marked a watershed in their plans for modernisation.

To gain an understanding of the artistic atmosphere that must have existed at the Mantuan court in the early 1460s, the account of the Veronese humanist Felice Feliciano's (1433–1479) trip made to Lake Garda with his humanist friends serves as a telling example. According to Feliciano, in September 1464 Mantegna, Samuele da Tradate – the son of the sculptor Jacopino – and Giovanni da Padova, who may be identified with the humanist Giovanni Marcanova (1410/18–1467), had visited the shores of the lake to look for antiquities and to read and discuss poetry.[7] Their outing reveals a desire not only to study the relics of the ancient Roman world, but to imaginatively recreate aspects of it, so much so that during the exploration Feliciano wore a garland of myrtle and ivy, and Samuele played the lute while sailing on the lake. This romantic approach to antiquity would manifest itself in many works by Mantegna, primarily the later *Triumphs of Caesar* (about 1485–1506) (discussed by Caroline Elam in this book), but would also inform his earliest paintings for the Gonzaga, in which classicising spaces are reconstructed in meticulous detail.

The first prestigious commission entrusted to Mantegna by Ludovico Gonzaga was probably intended as a testing ground: the decoration of the chapel of the Castello di San Giorgio, a fortified building at the core of the Gonzaga palace. The artist completed this assignment within the first half of the 1460s, displaying his skills in depicting classical architecture and feigned coloured marble, rocky landscapes and gloriously decorated garments, as well as foreshortened figures.[8] Although the chapel is unfortunately gone, some panels which Mantegna painted for it survive: they include the *Ascension*, the *Circumcision* and the

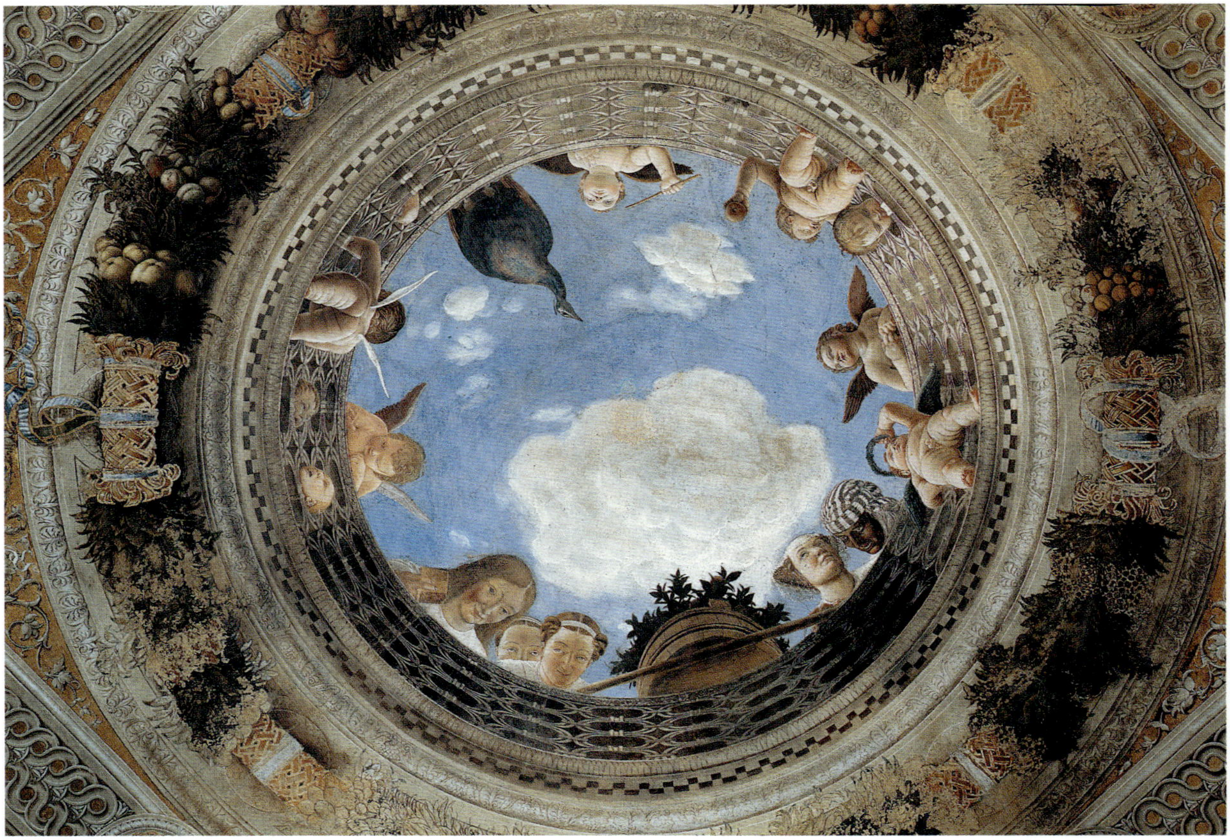

4 The oculus in the Camera degli Sposi, 1465–74
Fresco
Palazzo Ducale, Mantua

Adoration of the Magi in the Uffizi, Florence; a panel in the Prado, Madrid, representing the *Death of the Virgin* (fig. 3); and a small painting in the Pinacoteca Nazionale of Ferrara, with Christ welcoming the soul of the Madonna in heaven, which is a fragment of the Madrid painting.[9] These panels were probably fitted into a wooden frame or wainscoting in the small space designed for the marquis's private devotion.

The artist here indulges himself in depicting the scenes in minute detail, suggesting that the paintings were to be experienced slowly and at close range, paying attention to the nuances of materials and costumes. In the Madrid panel, moreover, reality and sacred history merge as the large window behind the Virgin's body shows the lake formed by the Mincio river and the bridge of San Giorgio, which spanned the water just outside the castle itself, as it still does today. The juxtaposition of painterly representation and topographical accuracy would have stimulated devout reflections on the immanence of religious mysteries.

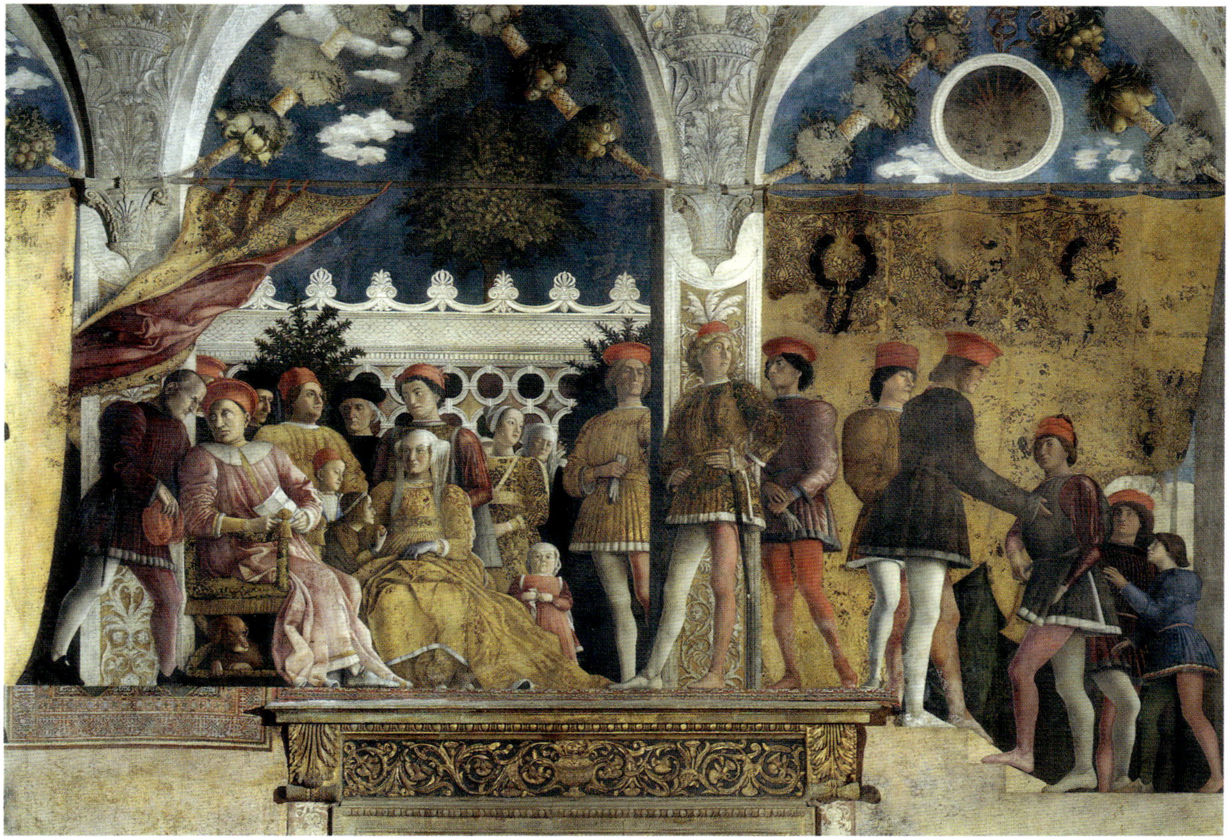

5 The northern wall in the Camera degli Sposi, 1465–74
Fresco
Palazzo Ducale, Mantua

The *camera picta*: a portrait of the Gonzaga court

Without a doubt Mantegna exceeded the Gonzaga's expectations and from then onwards they turned to him to paint their portraits, to execute paintings that they would use as diplomatic gifts and to decorate the most prestigious rooms of their residences. Among these, by far the most famous is the so-called Camera degli Sposi in the Castello di San Giorgio. Mantegna spent about a decade, from 1465 to 1474, decorating this almost cubic room. Known at the time as a *camera picta* (painted chamber) and already described in 1475 as 'the most beautiful room in the world', it was Marquis Ludovico's bedroom, but was also shown to important visitors and used as a reception room; it was only in the mid-seventeenth century that it came to be described as the room 'of the spouses'.[10]

According to the practice of the time, the artist started the work from the ceiling. Here, among festoons and putti, are scenes inspired by mythology, and eight

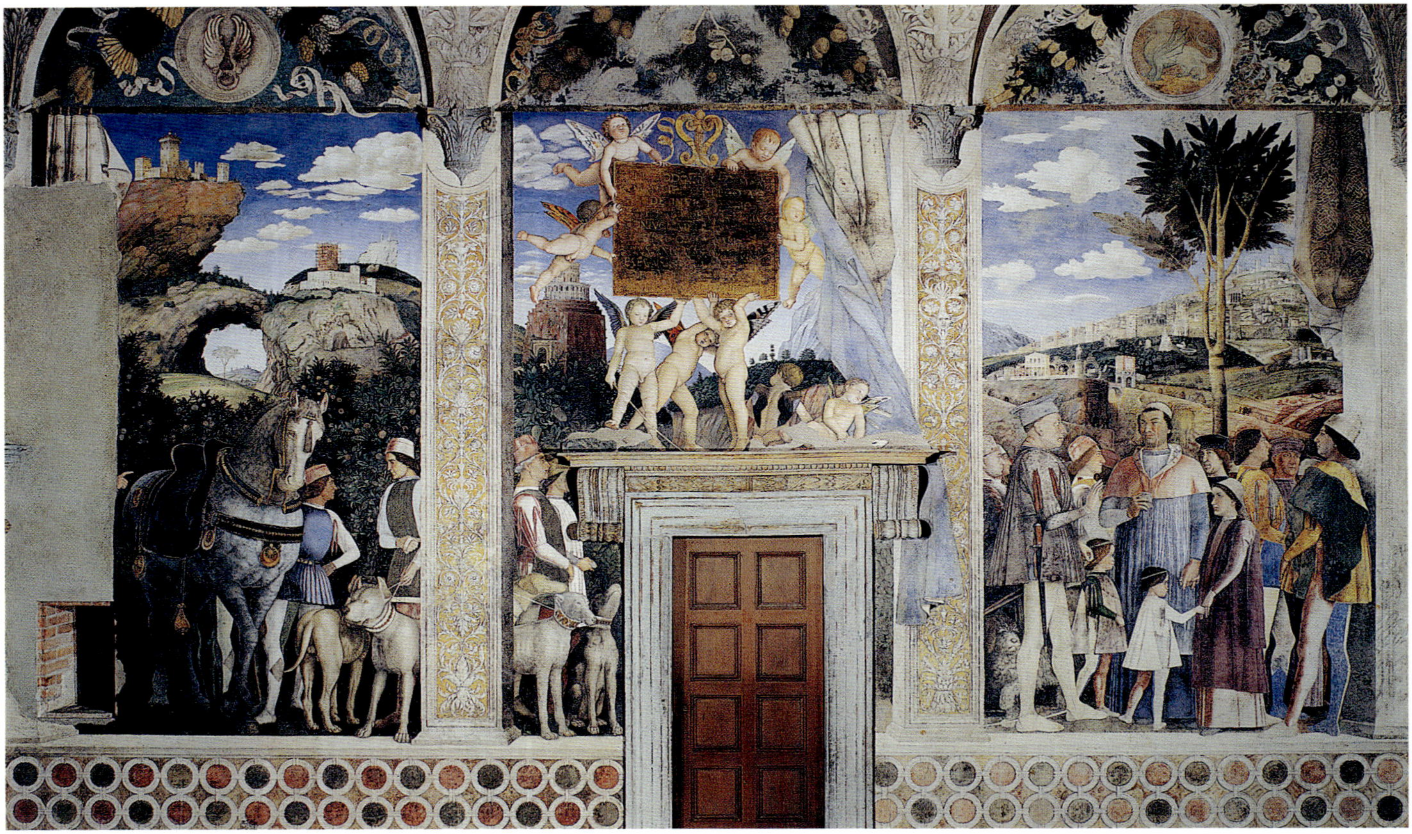

medallions with busts of Roman emperors. At the centre of the vault is the famous oculus (fig. 4), a fictive round opening inspired by the Pantheon in Rome, through which we see the blue sky, clouds and, foreshortened, a large vase of flowers, a peacock, ten playful putti and a group of court maids.

Below the ceiling, Mantegna imagined breaking through the walls to create a fictional space inhabited by the lord himself, his family and his retinue. These are some of the most memorable images of fifteenth-century Italy. On the northern wall (fig. 5), the court is represented in a moment of relaxed business: Marquis Ludovico is seated and rather casually consults an advisor with a sharp profile; next to him sits his German wife, Barbara of Brandenburg (hence the room 'of the spouses'), with their children. Around the ruling family gather members of an elegant entourage: one looks a little sad, others stand idle, one looks haughtily at the new arrivals emerging from the right. Early visitors to the room would have recognised the painted portraits of the lords and their closest courtiers. The scene, viewed slightly from below, seems to take place on a theatrical stage mounted in a garden with potted plants and enclosed by a wall encrusted with polychrome marbles. On the western wall (fig. 6), Mantegna painted two additional courtly scenes: the meeting of Ludovico

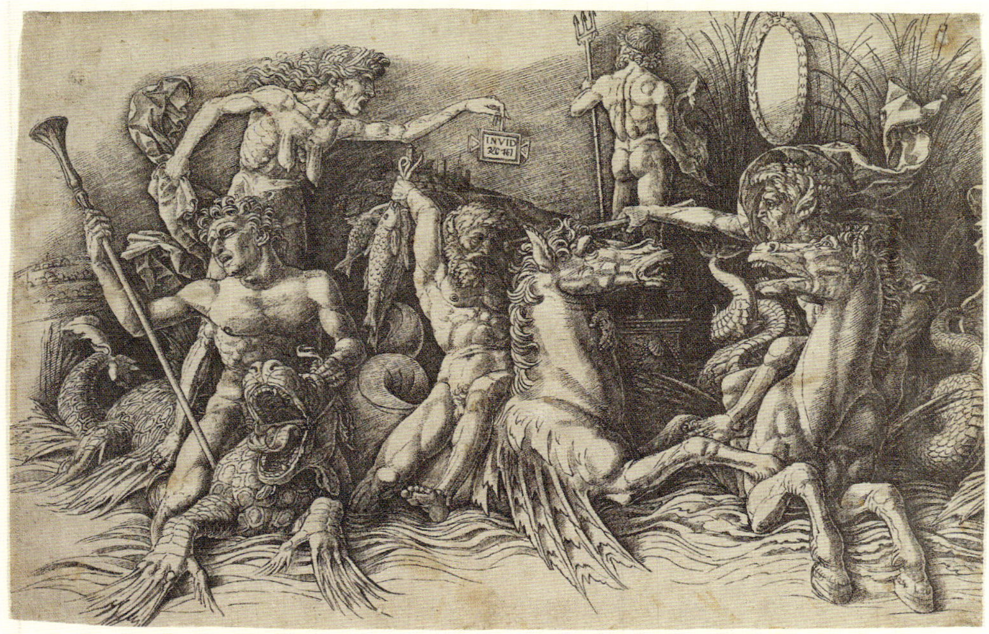

LEFT:
6 The western wall in the Camera degli Sposi, 1465–74
Fresco
Palazzo Ducale, Mantua

RIGHT:
7 *Battle of Sea Gods*, about 1475–1500
Engraving, 28.5 × 43 cm
The Metropolitan Museum of Art, New York. Rogers Fund, 1918 (18.12)

with his son Francesco, who had recently been made a cardinal and, on the left, a group of servants awaiting the marquis with a pair of magnificent dogs and an imposing horse adorned with golden harnesses. In the background of the first scene, a vast landscape opens up, with an imaginative vision of Rome on the slopes of a hill. There, alongside temples and ruins, one recognises Hadrian's mausoleum, a pyramid and a statue of Hercules on a high pedestal. Around the city, Mantegna, with the precision of a miniaturist, painted a countryside teeming with life: tiny figures are busy giving shape to stone blocks and columns, which perhaps recalled the contemporary building site of the Mantuan Church of Sant'Andrea designed by Alberti.[11] Standing on the door that divides the two episodes, three winged cherubs hold up the inscription with which the artist dedicated his work to Ludovico ('*opus hoc tenue*' or 'this subtle work').

Confirmed in his success, Mantegna obtained the title of count palatine and assumed the air of a lord: he began to collect antiquities, devoted himself to reading and formed a library with the major classical authors.[12] At this stage in his career, Mantegna also promoted the diffusion of his compositions through prints, feeding specially made drawings to an expert goldsmith and long-time collaborator, Gian Marco Cavalli (around 1454–after 1508).[13] Free from pre-established conventions and the constraints imposed by his patrons, in this field Mantegna let his imagination loose, inventing memorable Bacchic feasts and furious battles of sea gods (fig. 7). These became famous all across Europe, establishing his fame and legacy. Around 1476, at the height of his success, he began the construction of a large and modern house, which no artist before him could have aspired to own. The building, which was almost certainly designed by Mantegna himself, stands out for the originality of

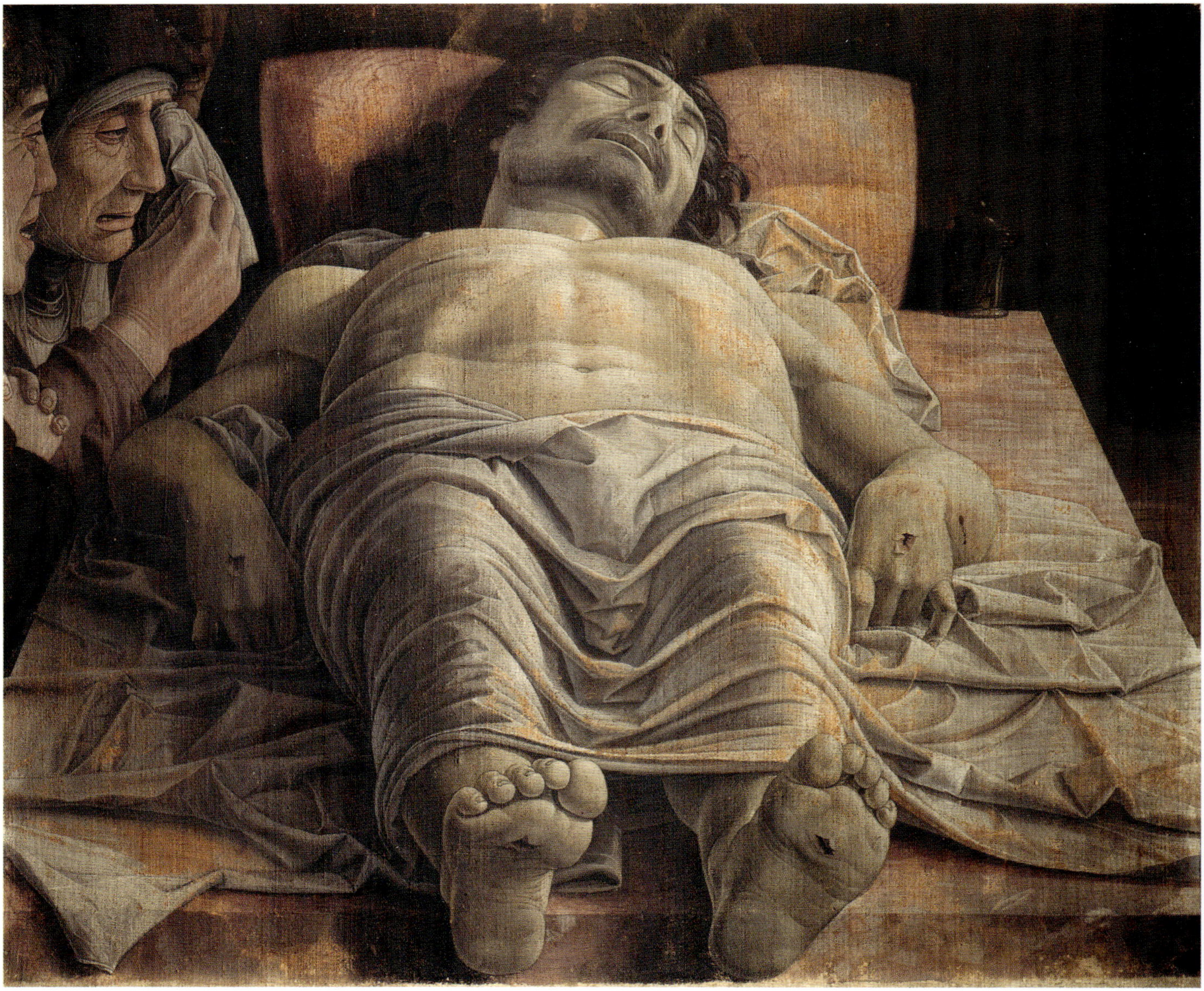

8 *Lamentation over the Dead Christ*, about 1483
Tempera on canvas, 68 × 81 cm
Pinacoteca di Brera, Milan

its circular courtyard inscribed in the compact cubic volume of the building. His ambition, however, proved to be hubristic and, unable to meet the expenses necessary to complete it, in 1502 he was forced to cede the building to the Gonzaga.[14]

Francesco II Gonzaga and the invention of antiquity

During the brief reign of Federico I Gonzaga who ruled from 1478 to 1484, Mantegna did not receive any major commission, but painted a number of daring paintings. These included the monumental *Saint Sebastian* in the Louvre, Paris (around 1480), which Chiara Gonzaga brought to France when she married Gilbert de Bourbon, Count of Montpensier in 1481; and the extraordinary *Dead Christ* in the Pinacoteca di Brera, Milan (fig. 8), also painted in the 1480s.[15] In the latter painting, the artist developed to an extreme level of sophistication his ability to render the foreshortened human body, with which he had experimented since his time in Padua, and repeatedly tested in works like *The Agony in the Garden* (see fig. 1) or the predella of the San Zeno altarpiece. In doing so, he possibly applied prescriptions by Leon Battista Alberti, who in his *De pictura* (1435) suggested the use of a transparent and squared veil to show bodies in space.[16] By then, Mantegna was admired well beyond Mantua. In 1482, Federico Duke of Urbino stopped to look at his paintings on a visit to Mantua, as reported in Giovanni Santi's *Cronaca* (1478–94): '[the Duke] had the greatest pleasure in admiring / The marvellous painting and the exalted art / Of Andrea Mantegna's high and famous genius ... Which flourishes in our outstanding age / Far more than others, Andrea bears the banner / Of its great excellent authority.'[17] Similarly, the following year, Lorenzo the Magnificent visited Mantegna's house, 'where he saw with great pleasure various paintings by the said Andrea, and certain sculpted heads and many other antique pieces, by which it seems he was much delighted'.[18]

Francesco II Gonzaga (ruled 1484–1519), son of Federico, engaged Mantegna in a long-term project, a series of nine large square canvases depicting *The Triumphs of Caesar* which exalted the military prowess of their patron. Here the antiquarian subject has been embellished by an exuberant repertoire of ancient objects and garments, partly imagined and partly drawn from ancient sources. Although the original destination of this imposing cycle is unclear, *The Triumphs of Caesar* contributed more than any other work to link Mantegna's name to Mantua and to establish the artist's fame. Mostly thanks to the *Triumphs*, Mantegna was one of the few fifteenth-century artists held in the highest esteem well into the sixteenth century, as shown by the praise given to him in the works of authors such as Baldassarre Castiglione (*The Book of the Courtier*, 1528), Ludovico Ariosto (*Orlando furioso*, 1532) and Giorgio Vasari (*The Lives of the Artists*, 1550).

Another important work created by Mantegna for Francesco II Gonzaga was the altarpiece known as the *Madonna della Vittoria* (fig. 9), painted to comply with the vow made by the marquis before the battle

BELOW:
9 *Madonna della Vittoria*, 1495–6
Tempera on canvas, 280 × 166 cm
Musée du Louvre, Paris

OPPOSITE:
10 *The Virgin and Child with Saints*, 1490s
Tempera on canvas, 139.1 × 116.8 cm
The National Gallery, London

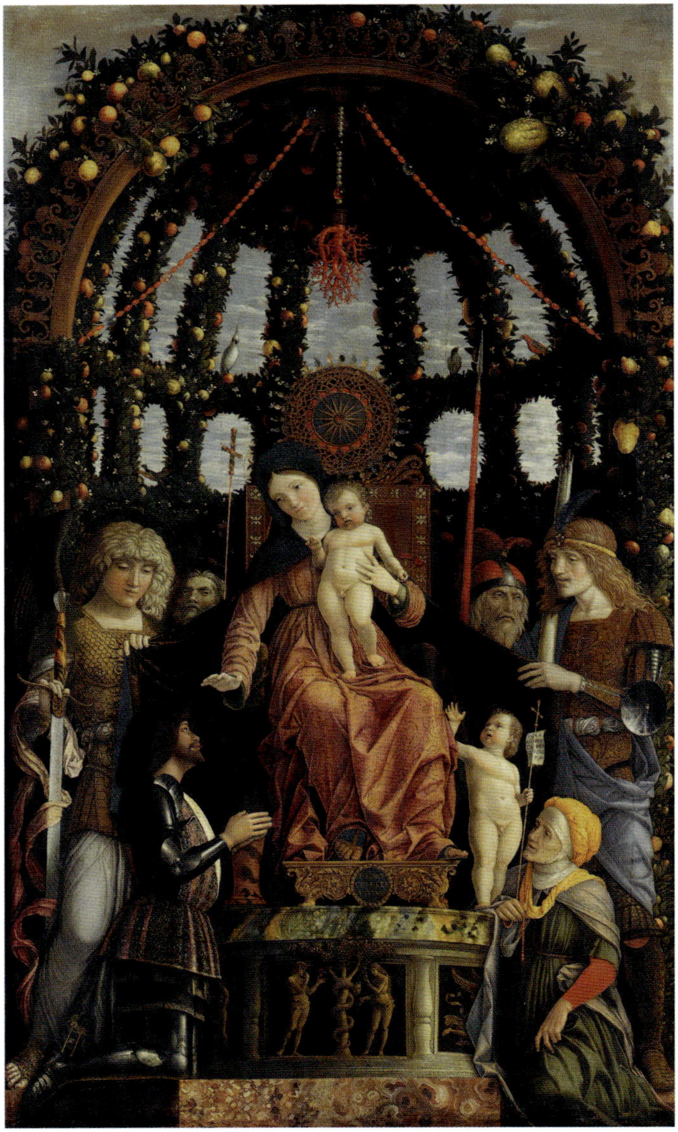

of Fornovo, which he won against the French army in 1495.[19] Although the victory was of dubious importance, Francesco used this event to build his image as a valiant military leader: he celebrated it by commissioning Mantegna's altarpiece and promoting the construction of a new church dedicated to Santa Maria della Vittoria to house it. Once completed, the altarpiece was paraded through the streets of Mantua and installed with great pomp in July 1496 on the high altar of the new building, where it stayed until 1797. In that year, French troops removed it and took it to the Louvre, where it remains to this day. In the painting, the Madonna and Child sit on a throne made of precious, coloured marbles, decorated with gold and embellished with transparent beads made of rock crystal. She turns towards the kneeling Marquis Francesco in armour, with a gesture of protection and blessing, welcoming him under her cloak held open by two warrior saints, Saint Michael and Saint George – an unusual version of the iconography of the Madonna of Mercy. In the background, Mantegna painted two locally venerated saints – Saint Andrew on the left and Saint Longinus on the right – while in the foreground are the infant Saint John the Baptist and an elderly woman, who may be Saint Elizabeth. The work's most extraordinary invention, however, destined to impress generations of young painters, is the pergola that frames the sacred scene, lush with flowers and fruit, and animated by a parrot, with a coral branch, symbol of death and resurrection, hanging in the centre.

Two paintings in the National Gallery, unusually executed on canvas, date from around this period:

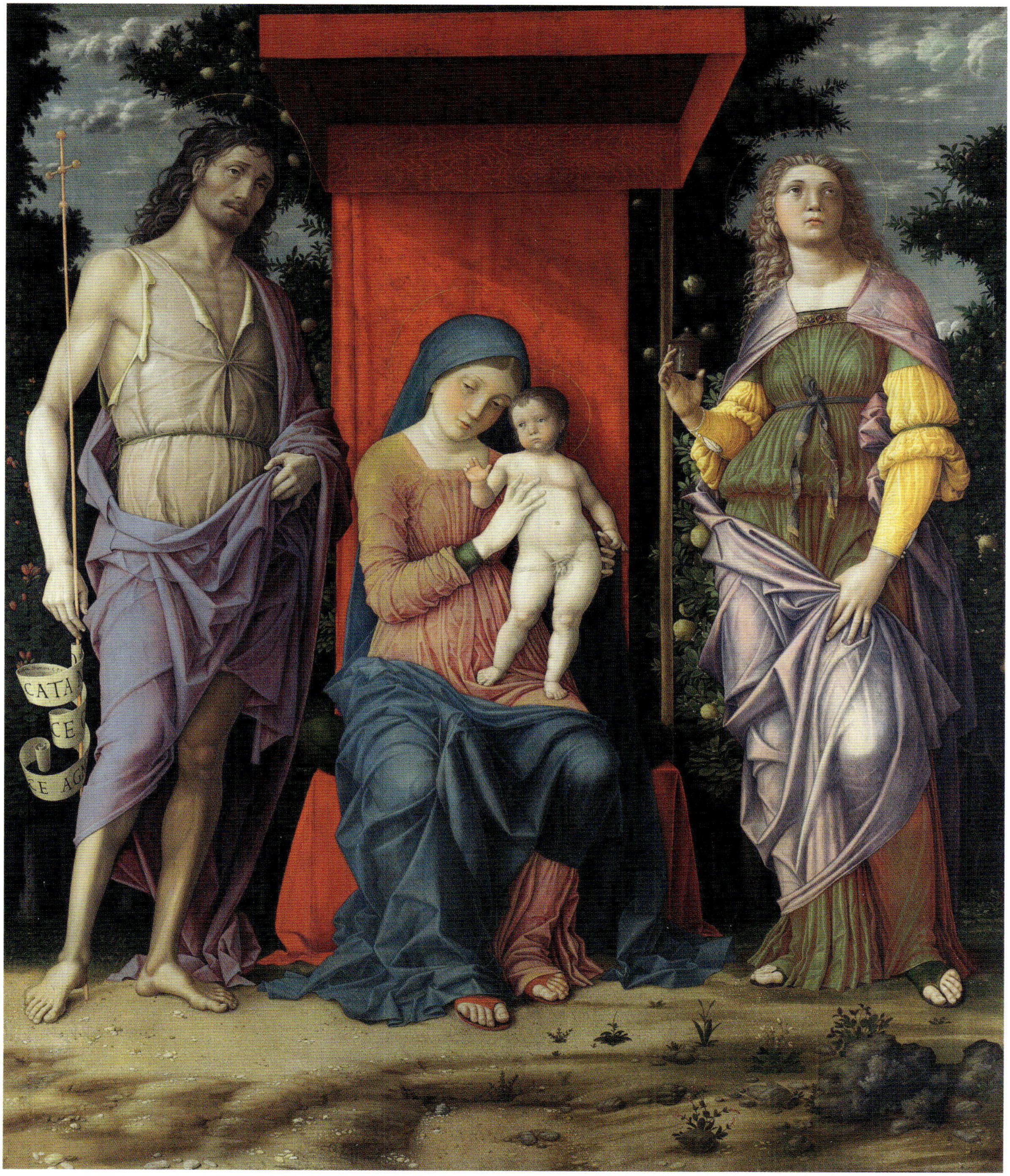
CATA
CE
E AG

11 *The Holy Family with Saint John the Baptist*, about 1500
Glue tempera on canvas, 71.1 × 50.8 cm
The National Gallery, London

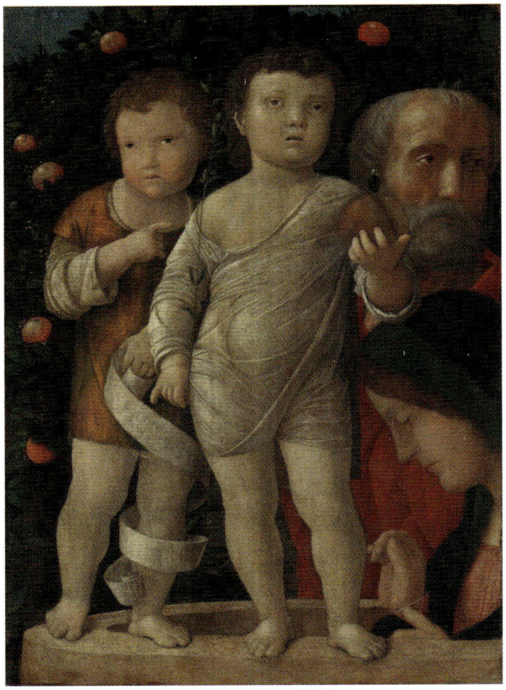

The Virgin and Child with Saints (fig. 10) and *The Holy Family with Saint John the Baptist* (fig. 11).[20] The first is a relatively small altarpiece painted for an unknown location and patron. Its canvas support suggests that it may have been intended to be displayed outside Mantua, as it could be rolled up and easily transported. Particularly notable in this painting is the sumptuously dressed figure of the Magdalen, who stands in *contrapposto* (with weight on one leg) like an ancient statue and exemplifies Mantegna's ability to blend the monumentality of classical statuary with meticulously observed forms. The smaller painting, surely executed for private devotion, is a representation of the young Jesus Christ, standing in the centre with an olive branch and the orb in his hands, symbols respectively of peace and universal authority.

In the service of Isabella d'Este

At the end of the fifteenth century, around the same time as the two above-mentioned paintings were created, Mantegna, now in his sixties, found himself at the service of the young and ambitious Isabella d'Este (1474–1539), daughter of the Duke of Ferrara, who married Marquis Francesco II in 1490.[21] Aged 17, Isabella entered the city in a painted carriage, passing under five triumphal arches. She settled in the Castello di San Giorgio, where, a few metres from the *camera picta*, a private apartment was reserved for her, consisting of two bedrooms and a series of small dressing rooms including an oratory, a library and the study, or studiolo, which would become an object of particular pride. At first, Isabella was content to decorate her studiolo with heraldic symbols and emblems. Soon, however, she made more ambitious plans for that small private space of hers dedicated to leisure, music and art.[22] Isabella surely remembered that her uncle Leonello d'Este had furnished a study in the suburban villa of Belfiore with a cycle of paintings representing the Muses. With that example in mind, after a prolonged visit to her father's court in 1495, Isabella decided to begin a radical renovation of her studiolo to project an image of herself as a learned, virtuous and exacting lady. She commissioned a series of paintings with edifying subjects from the best artists of the time: Mantegna, Pietro Perugino (1446–1523) and the Ferrarese Lorenzo Costa (1460–1535). Isabella also intended to have paintings made for her by Giovanni Bellini and Leonardo da Vinci (1452–1519), but these were never made. The first painting that Mantegna executed for Isabella's studiolo, between 1496 and 1497, was the so-called *Parnassus* (fig. 12). Mars and Venus dominate the space from the top of a natural arch, while the nine Muses in the foreground dance to the sound of Apollo's lyre. On the right, Mercury appears with Pegasus, his winged horse, and on the left, in the distance, Vulcan, Venus' husband, is busy hammering the fine net which he is preparing to trap and expose the adultery of his wife and her lover and so avenge his honour. Documents show that contemporaries interpreted the figure of Venus as Isabella d'Este, queen of a harmonious world, regulated by love and music. In the second painting executed by Mantegna, *Minerva expelling Vices from the Garden of Virtue* (fig. 13), completed in 1502, the personifications of vices, immersed up to their waists in a murky pond, are accompanied by identifying labels: Avarice, Ignorance, Ingratitude, Idleness and Fraud. Upon the arrival of Minerva, Diana and another figure who has been interpreted as Chastity, the vices depart, together with families of satyrs and a lascivious Venus, who stands naked on the back of a centaur. High above, behind perfectly pruned hedges, a mountain of orange rock rises under an anthropomorphic cloud while, in a disc of vapours, Justice, Strength and Temperance await Minerva's fulfilment of her task. At the time of his death on 13 September 1506, Mantegna was working on his third painting for the series, depicting the *Kingdom of the God Comus*, an unusual subject that the master left at a preliminary stage and which was only completed around 1511 by Lorenzo Costa, the painter who, after Mantegna's death, and before the arrival of Giulio Romano (1499?–1546) in 1524, enjoyed a privileged place at the Gonzaga court.

These paintings ennobled a room used for reading, playing music, leisure and display to important guests. Accounts of Isabella's sophisticated study and its treasures began to circulate early on, presenting the room and its precious contents as a portrait of the virtues and ambitions of their owner. Like Mantegna, Isabella was fascinated by antiquities and collected them from all around the Mediterranean, alongside precious modern works which she displayed in an adjacent and equally small room, called the Grotta (grotto), which was dedicated to housing her collections.[23] In 1504, she even managed to extort a marble head of the Roman Empress Faustina from Mantegna himself at a time when he was in financial difficulties over expenditure on his house.[24]

Three works by Mantegna in the National Gallery illustrate well the fascination with antiquity felt by Isabella and Mantegna himself. These are painted in

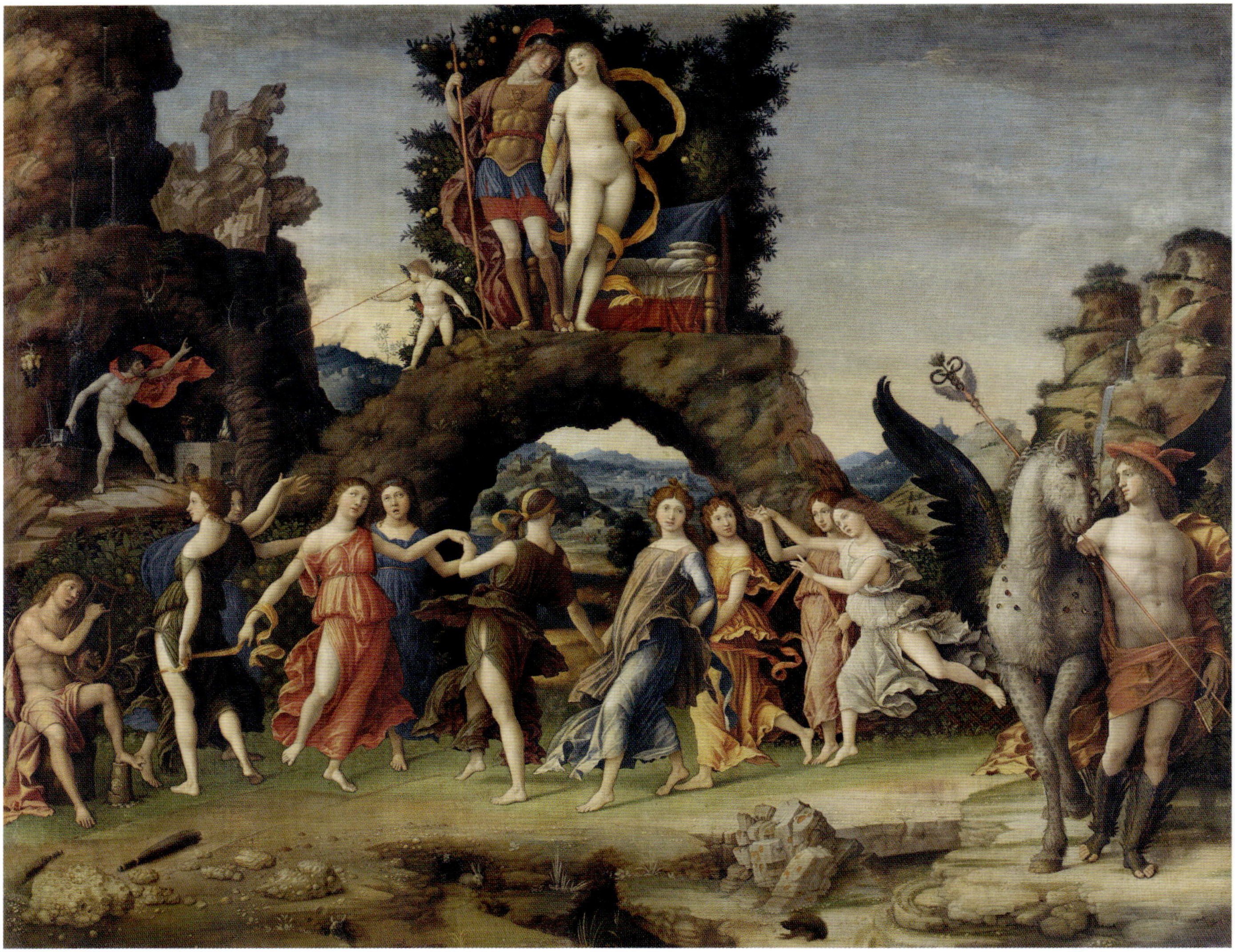

12 *Parnassus*, about 1496–7
Tempera on canvas, 148 × 182 cm (original canvas)
Musée du Louvre, Paris

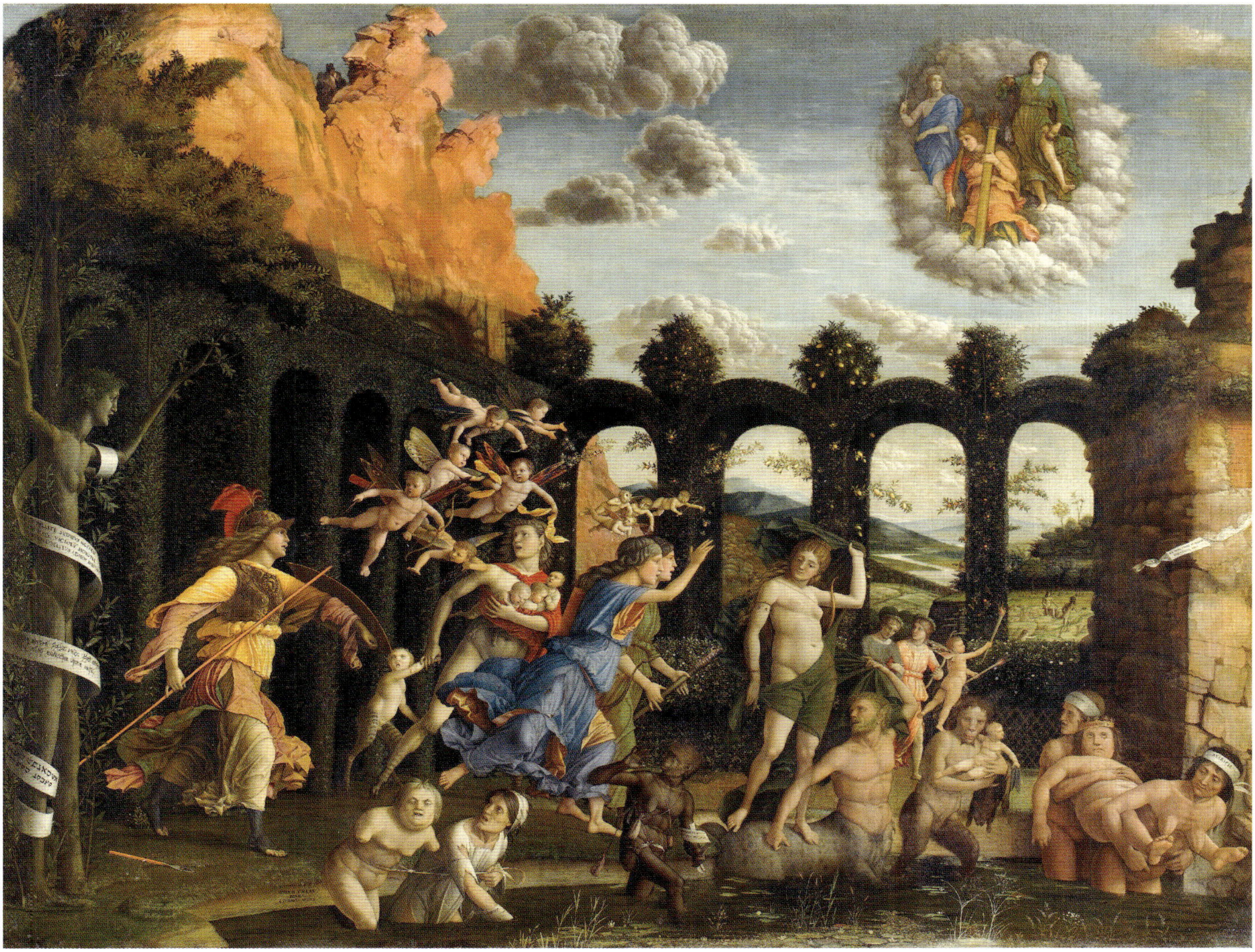

13 *Minerva expelling Vices from the Garden of Virtue*, 1502
Tempera on canvas, 149 × 189 cm (original canvas)
Musée du Louvre, Paris

BELOW LEFT:
14 *The Vestal Virgin Tuccia with a Sieve*, about 1495–1506
Tempera on poplar, 72.5 × 23 cm
The National Gallery, London

BELOW RIGHT:
15 *A Woman drinking (Sophonisba?)*, about 1495–1506
Tempera on poplar, 71.2 × 19.8 cm
The National Gallery, London

OPPOSITE:
16 *The Introduction of the Cult of Cybele at Rome*, 1505–6
Glue tempera on canvas, 76.5 × 273 cm
The National Gallery, London

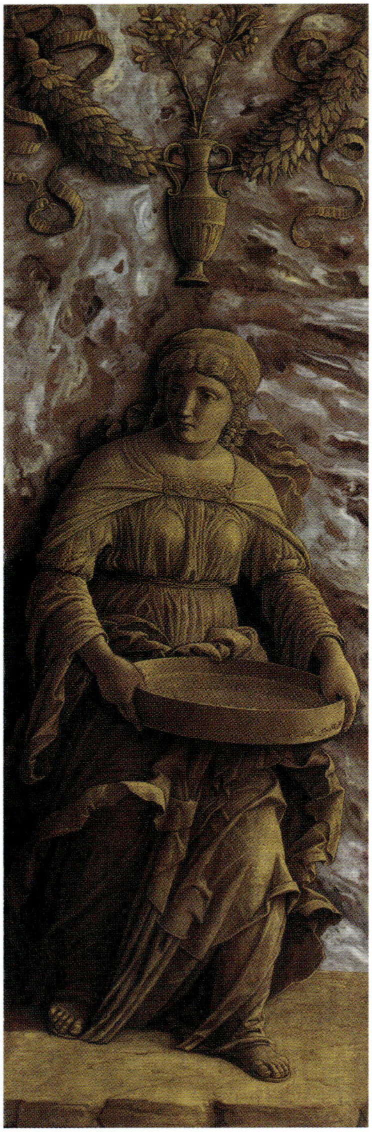

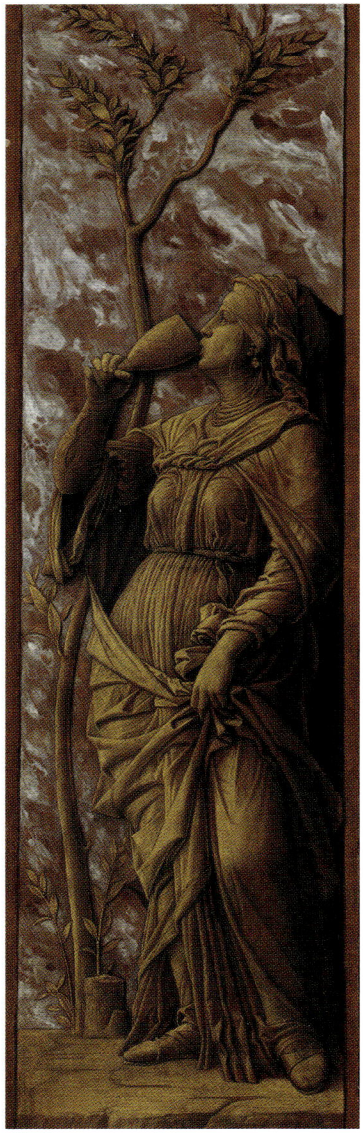

monochrome as if they were feigned marble or bronze reliefs set against a background of coloured marbles. They all show ancient or biblical female figures and have therefore been related to the patronage of Isabella d'Este, who indeed had two similar paintings in her studiolo, listed after her death in 1539. Of the three works in the National Gallery, two represent heroic women from Roman history: the Vestal Tuccia who miraculously carried water in a sieve from the river Tiber to the temple of Vesta to prove her virginity (fig. 14) and a woman drinking from a chalice, perhaps the Carthaginian princess Sophonisba who drank poison rather than be paraded as prisoner through Rome (fig. 15). The third painting, on canvas, depicts *Samson and Delilah*, a story of deception in which Delilah seduces the Israelite Samson and then deprives him of his strength by cutting his hair while asleep.[25] Several such paintings by Mantegna imitating ancient reliefs survive.[26] They were all probably meant to decorate sumptuous rooms like Isabella's studiolo and offered the artist the opportunity to show off his mimetic skills and to test the limits of painting in the creation of illusionistic depictions of other materials. Such was the appeal of these works that in 1505 a Venetian patrician, Francesco Cornaro, who claimed to be heir of the ancient Roman *gens Cornelia* (Cornelia family), was allowed to commission from Mantegna, for his study, four multi-figural friezes representing the deeds of his supposed ancestors. Before his death in 1506, Mantegna had painted only *The Introduction of the Cult of Cybele at Rome* (fig. 16), a magnificent

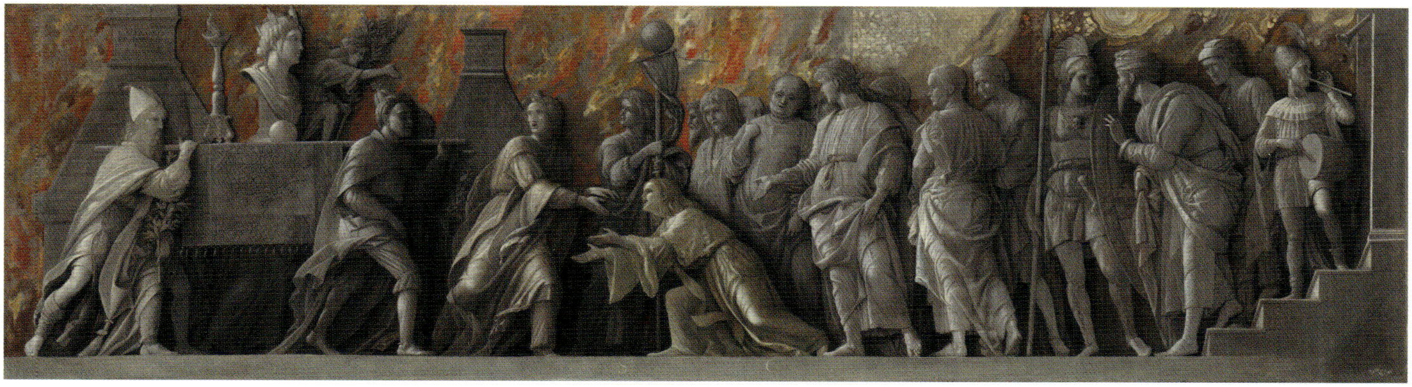

painting in grisaille depicting the entry into Rome of the statue of Cybele which Publius Cornelius Scipio Nasica brought from Anatolia. When Mantegna died, leaving the commission incomplete, Cornaro resorted to Giovanni Bellini, who painted for him the *Continence of Publius Cornelius Scipio* in a long frieze also in grisaille (National Gallery of Art, Washington).[27] Mantegna's prestige in Venice was at its highest at the time of Cornaro's commission, and he is known to have invited Albrecht Dürer to meet him in Mantua. Dürer, then in Venice, accepted the invitation, only to find that Mantegna had died before he could join him. A testament to Dürer's appreciation of Mantegna's work survives in his carefully copied pen and ink drawing after the prints of the *Battle of the Sea Gods*.[28]

While engaged in the commissions for Isabella and Cornaro, in 1504 Mantegna began to think about his death and the foundation of a funerary chapel worthy of the high status he had achieved.[29] To this end, he acquired the patronage of the first nave chapel on the left of the church of Sant'Andrea and, with his son, the painter Francesco Mantegna (around 1470–1517), decorated the vault with a fictive pergola framing the family coat of arms. For the same space, he painted an altarpiece, now ruined, representing the *Baptism of Christ* and a *Holy Family with the Family of Saint John the Baptist*, both still *in situ*. Only after the artist's death, in September 1506, did the chapel reach its definitive structure, thanks to the intervention of Francesco Mantegna and the young Correggio (active 1494–1534), to whom at least two of the evangelists frescoed in the spandrels are traditionally attributed.[30] The chapel also houses a magnificent bronze bust of Mantegna set against a porphyry disc, perhaps created by the goldsmith Gian Marco Cavalli, who worked alongside Mantegna in Mantua from at least 1475 until the artist's last days.[31]

By the time of his death, Mantegna had dominated artistic production in Mantua for over 40 years and turned his adoptive city into a creative centre, attracting artists and collectors eager to see or possess works by him. Used as diplomatic gifts, his paintings were coveted by aristocrats in France, Germany and Spain. In 1499, for instance, Cardinal Georges d'Amboise, the main advisor to the French King Louis XII, was reported to consider Mantegna 'the first painter in the world' and to have wished 'to pay any amount to possess something by him'.[32] In this way, Mantegna's art significantly contributed to turning a provincial city and a minor dynasty, the Gonzaga, into exemplars of taste at the forefront of artistic developments.

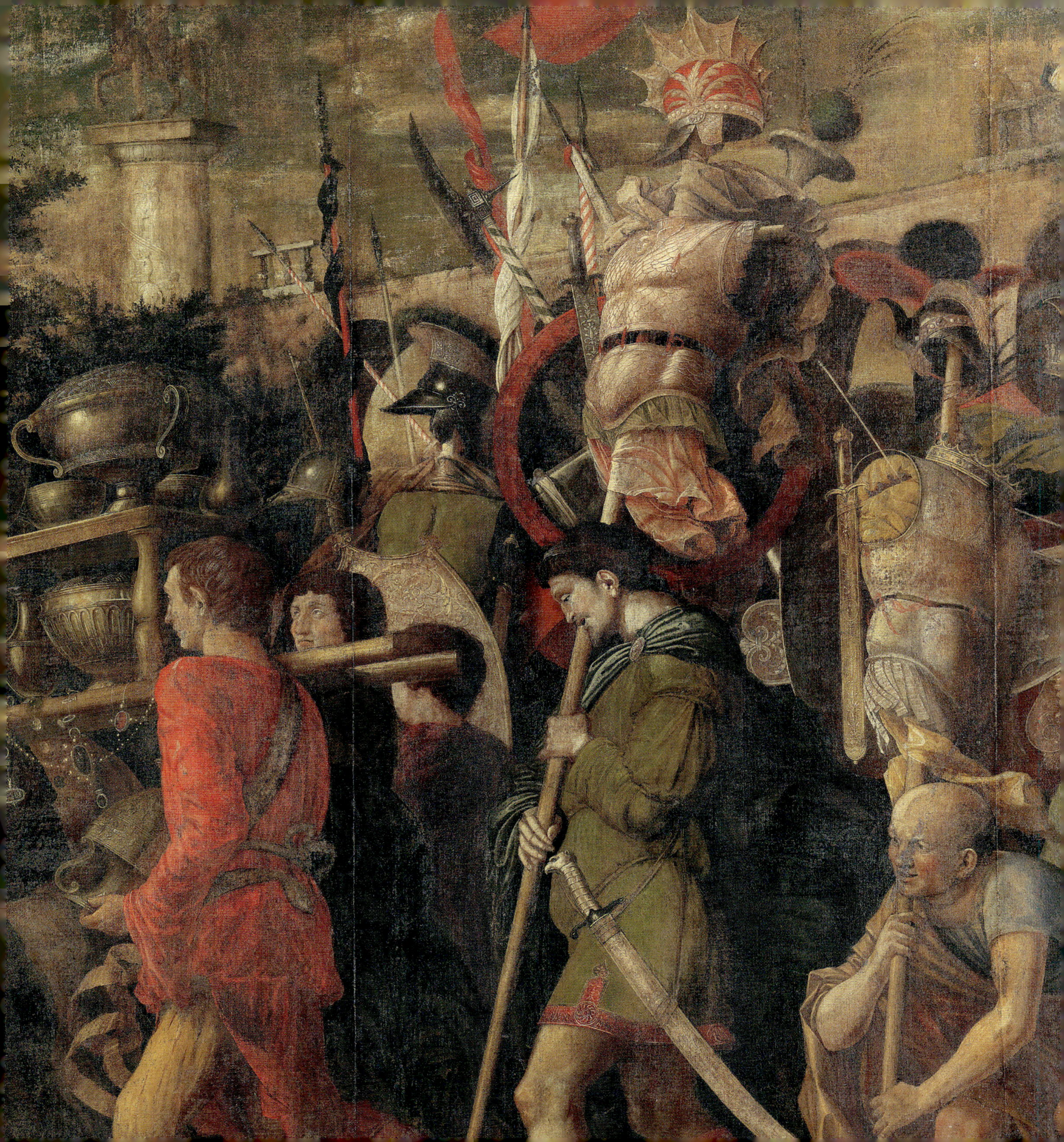

MANTEGNA'S TRIUMPHS: FORM AND LIFE

CAROLINE ELAM

In truth, I am not ashamed of having made them, and I still have hopes of making others.

Andrea Mantegna in a letter to Marquis Francesco Gonzaga, 31 January 1489[1]

Andrea Mantegna's nine canvases of the *Triumphs of Caesar* were, in his lifetime and for centuries after his death, considered to be the artist's finest achievement.[2] The most brilliant visual reconstruction of a Roman triumph ever attempted, they are still the central images used by classicists to evoke such processions.[3] Although the vulnerable technique of tempera on canvas, the depredations caused by travel to England in the seventeenth century and the misguided restorations in the past have made them shadows of what they once were, they nonetheless still convey an overwhelming sense of epic grandeur on the move.[4] Acquired with the rest of the Gonzaga collection in Mantua by Charles I in 1629, the canvases were spared from the sale of the royal art treasures under the Commonwealth, and have remained at Hampton Court Palace ever since (see Director's Foreword).[5]

Despite the fame of the *Triumphs*, the contemporary evidence for them is sparse. We do not know when Mantegna began or finished work on them, which of the Gonzaga marquises commissioned them, in which palace or room the sequence of nine canvases, all lit from the left, was intended to hang, or whether the series is complete as it stands. A suggestion that the original patron was Marquis Ludovico Gonzaga (ruled 1444–78), shortly after the completion in 1474 of Mantegna's celebrated *camera picta* (the so-called Camera degli Sposi) in the Castello di San Giorgio, has not found general favour.[6] The first mention of

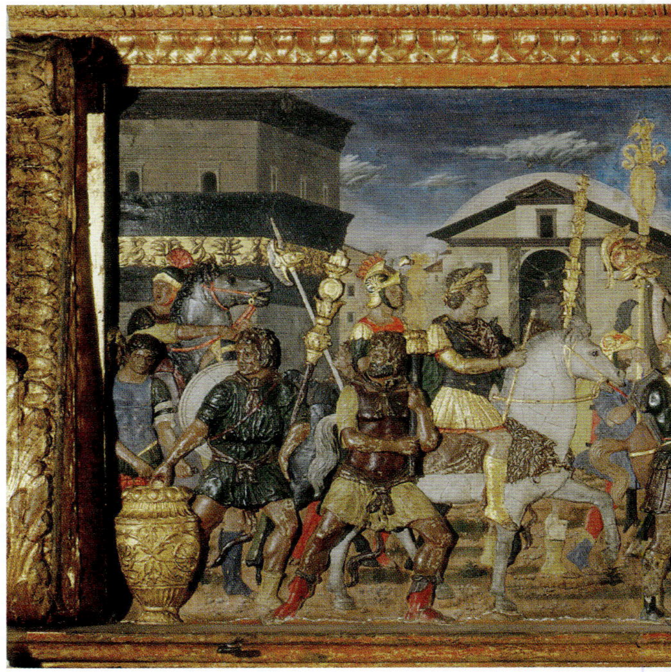

1 Unknown Mantuan artist
Justice of Trajan, 1477
One of a pair of chests with painted gesso low reliefs, 67 × 212 cm
Landesmuseum, Klagenfurt

Mantegna at work on the *Triumphs* (in the plural) comes from 1486, when the teenage Duke of Urbino enjoyed seeing them on a visit to Mantua,[7] and most writers have concluded that they were commissioned by Francesco II Gonzaga (1466–1519) soon after his accession in 1484. Certainly he came to support the project wholeheartedly, referring in 1492 to the 'Triumph of Julius Caesar which [Mantegna] is now painting for us with such nearly living and breathing images that it seems not to be a representation but a living thing'.[8] It was Francesco who in 1506–8 had a room custom-built to accommodate the canvases in his new Palazzo di San Sebastiano near Alberti's church of that name.[9] It is not to be excluded that the *Triumphs* project was initiated by Federico I Gonzaga (ruled 1478–84), who was protective of Mantegna, had some military pretensions and was building an ambitious new palace (the Domus Nova).[10] However, all the Gonzaga marquises were military men and all stood to gain by association with the first of the Caesars, the most successful general of the Roman world. And, in the last analysis, the canvases were and always would be seen as Mantegna's; the artist himself called them 'my Triumphs'.[11]

Triumphal imagery was ubiquitous in fifteenth-century secular art and ritual, but no artist before Mantegna had attempted a large-scale depiction of a complete Roman triumph in many scenes. Petrarch's allegorical *Trionfi* (a subject also tackled by Mantegna's entourage) constitute a separate tradition.[12] Roman subjects including processions of ancient Roman generals sometimes figure on fifteenth-century cassoni (marriage chests), but are usually depicted with anachronistic style and costumes. One notable exception is the pair of chests with painted gesso low reliefs of the *Justice of Trajan* (Landesmuseum, Klagenfurt) made in Mantua for the wedding of Paola Gonzaga with Leonhard Count of Görz in 1477 (fig. 1).[13] Although surely not designed by the artist himself, these are strongly Mantegnesque in their figure style and archaeological detailing, and evoke the cultural climate from which the *Triumphs* emerged. This relates to a whole north Italian tradition of fresco cycles and manuscripts going back to the fourteenth century. We are told that Mantegna admired the triumphs painted by Jacopo Avanzi in the Scaliger palace in Verona, and their humour and poignancy remained in his mind when he worked on his *Captives* canvas.[14] Also relevant to Mantegna's visual thinking are certain

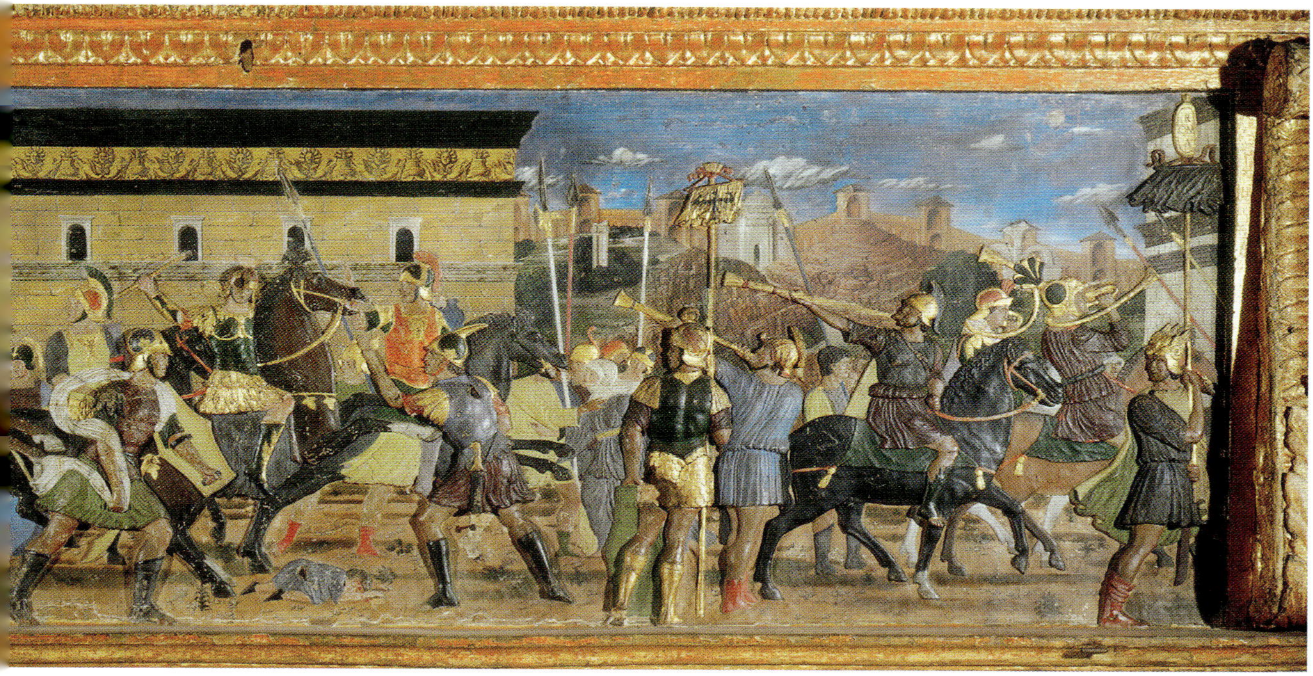

north Italian manuscript illuminations of classical, Petrarchan or epigraphic texts, such as the triumphal scene illustrating his antiquarian friend Giovanni Marcanova's *Collectio Antiquitatum* of 1465, or the miniaturist Gaspare da Padova's brilliant *all'antica* inventions in his manuscript illuminations.[15] All these are more archaeologically ambitious than any central Italian precedents. Large paintings on canvas are sometimes viewed as inexpensive alternatives to costly and prestigious tapestries, and the only precedent in Mantua for a series of large-scale representations of Roman history was four tapestries of the history of Hannibal and Scipio Africanus, now lost, which were apparently woven for Ludovico Gonzaga.[16] It may be significant that Mantegna's *Triumphs* were selectively used on occasion for temporary court festivities and theatrical performances. The decision to paint on canvas made them deployable in this way, but canvas had long been a support favoured by the artist and one he increasingly preferred.[17]

The quadruple triumph on successive days awarded to Julius Caesar in 46 BC celebrated his victories over Gaul, Egypt, Pontus (a kingdom on the Black Sea in present-day Turkey) and Africa (against Juba, King of Numidia). Mantegna settled finally on one of these in particular: the Gallic triumph. The second canvas has an inscription including the phrase 'OB GALLIAM DEVICT[AM]' (on account of the defeat of Gaul) while a preliminary design for the first (fig. 2) proclaims 'GALIA CAPTA' (Gaul taken). However, at first he may have intended a composite representation of several different triumphs, since Canvas 9, showing Caesar on his triumphal chariot, features a garland inscribed with his celebrated boast 'VENI VIDI VICI' (I came, I saw,

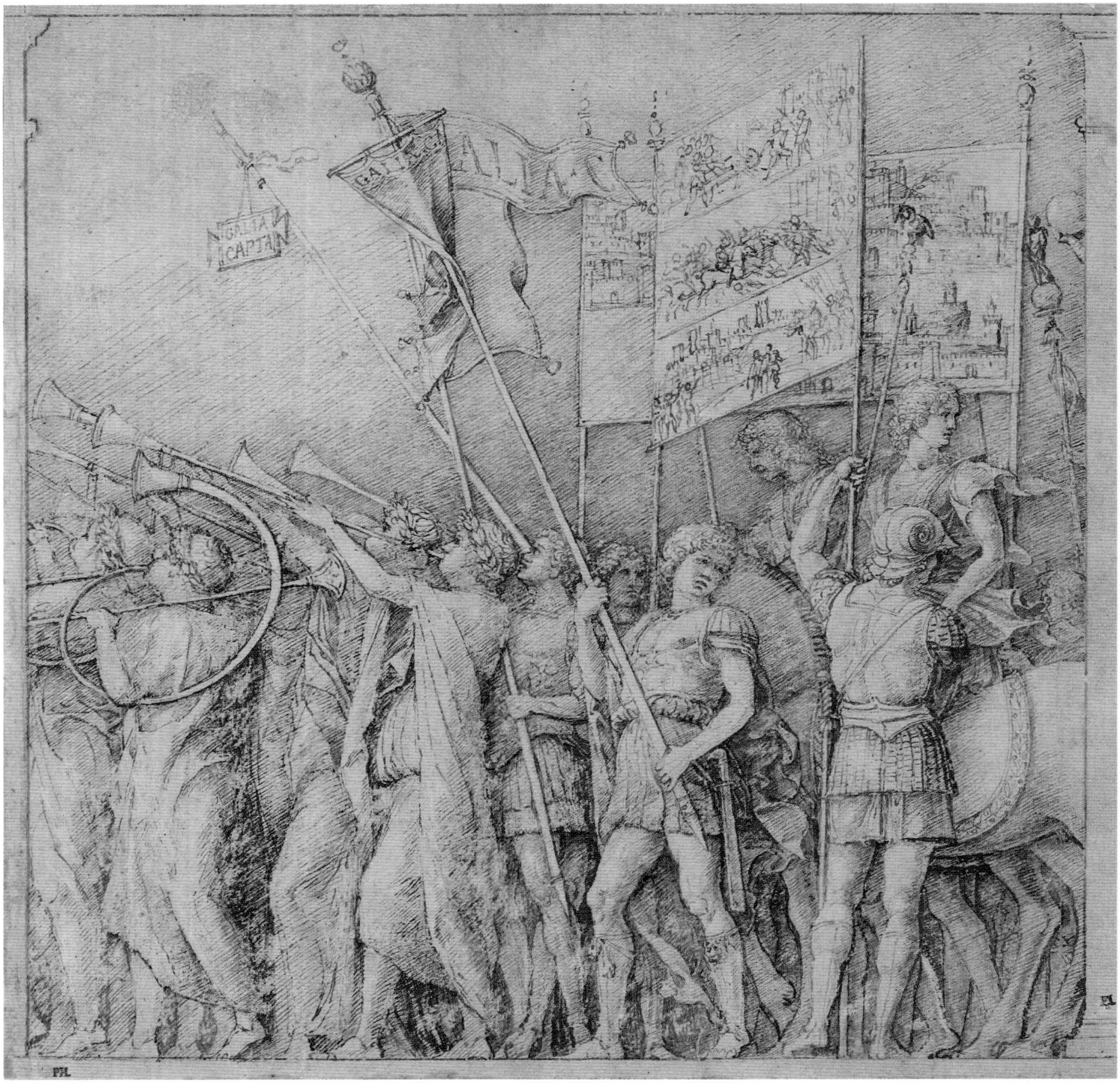

2 Workshop of Mantegna
Copy of preliminary study for Canvas 1,
The Trumpeters, late fifteenth century
Pen and brown ink on paper (laid down), 27.5 × 27.6 cm
Rothschild collection, Musée du Louvre, Paris

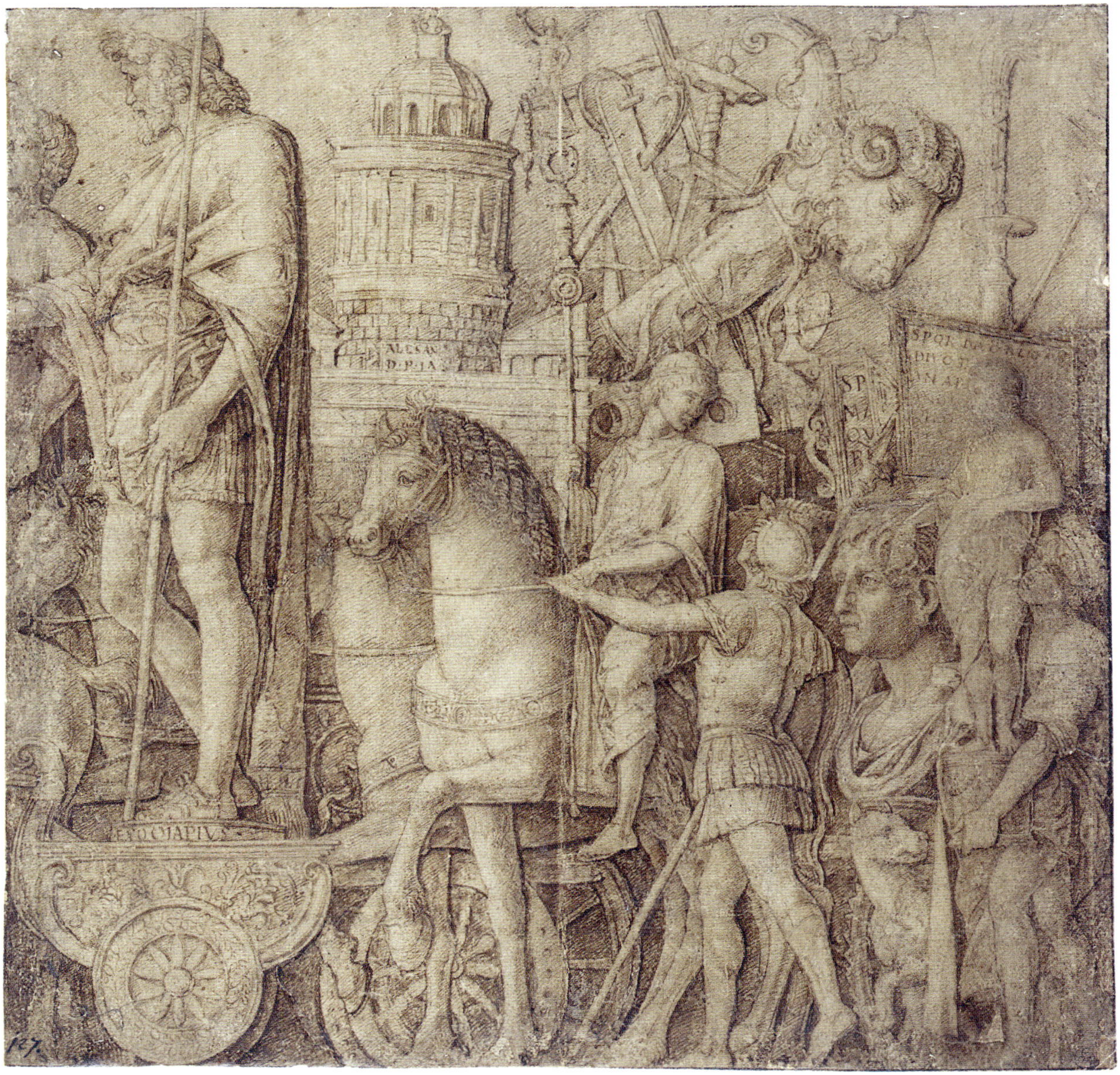

3 Attributed to Mantegna
Copy of preliminary study for Canvas 2,
The Triumphal Carts, late fifteenth century
Pen and brown ink on paper, 26.6 × 26.6 cm
Private collection

BELOW:
4 Sculptural reliefs of triumphal procession from the Arch of Trajan at Benevento, southern Italy, second century AD
Marble

OPPOSITE:
5 Sculptural relief of triumphal procession (carrying the menorah) from the Arch of Titus, Rome, first century AD
Marble

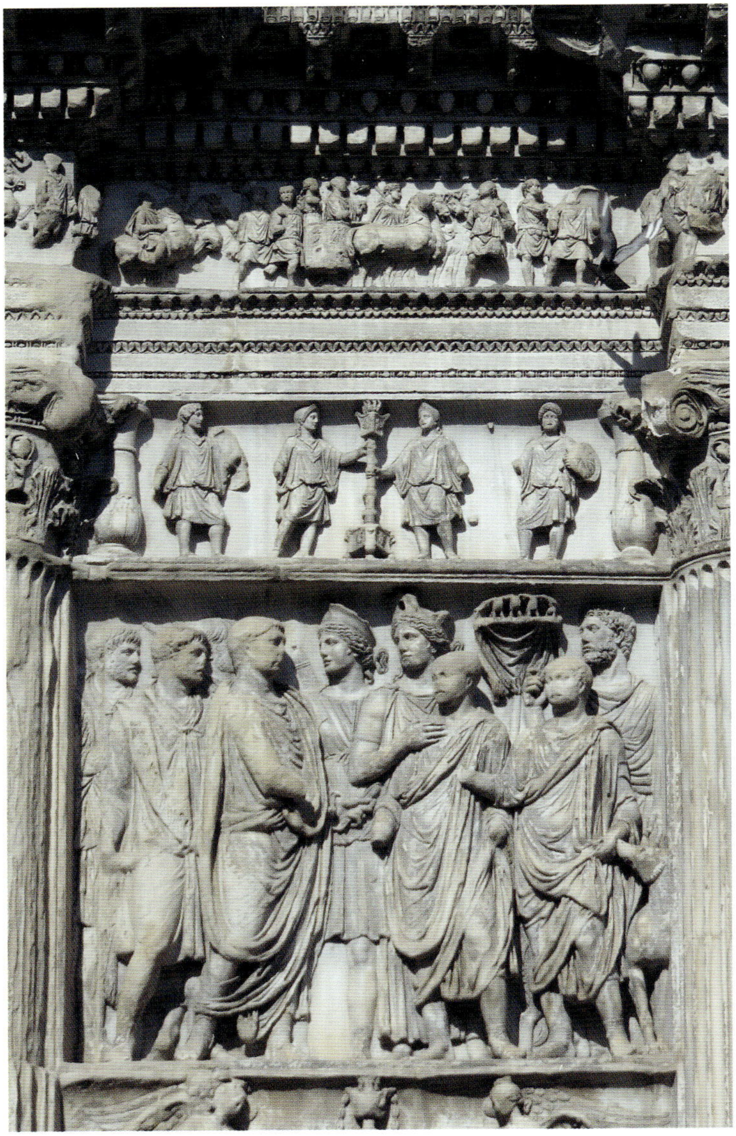

I conquered), pithily conveying the lightning speed of his Pontic campaign,[18] and a recently discovered drawing associated with Canvas 2 (fig. 3) seems to make reference to the Egyptian city of Alexandria.[19]

Though famous, Caesar's 46 BC triumphs do not figure in surviving ancient art, nor are they described in much detail by ancient historians.[20] Mantegna, presumably helped by humanist scholars, used as reference material the detailed descriptions in the ancient sources of triumphs awarded to other generals; but he and his advisers are likely to have turned first to contemporary antiquarian writings, such as the lost treatise by Marcanova, already mentioned, and the comprehensive accounts to be found in Book X of Flavio Biondo's *Roma Triumphans*, which may indeed have done much to inspire the project.[21] Biondo (1392–1463) completed his work at the Congress of Mantua in 1459, organised to promote a crusade, and he dedicated it to Pope Pius II, the instigator of that event. The following year he complied with Ludovico's request for a manuscript of the work and its first edition was among the earliest books to be printed in Mantua in around 1472. In the tenth book of this study of Roman institutions, Biondo effectively provided a chronologically organised guide to the ancient writings that described triumphs, which could then be separately consulted in detail. The fullest accounts of the order and content of triumphal processions are in Appian's and Plutarch's descriptions of the triumphs of Scipio Africanus and Aemilius Paulus.[22] Surviving visual representations of Roman triumphs were few, the most

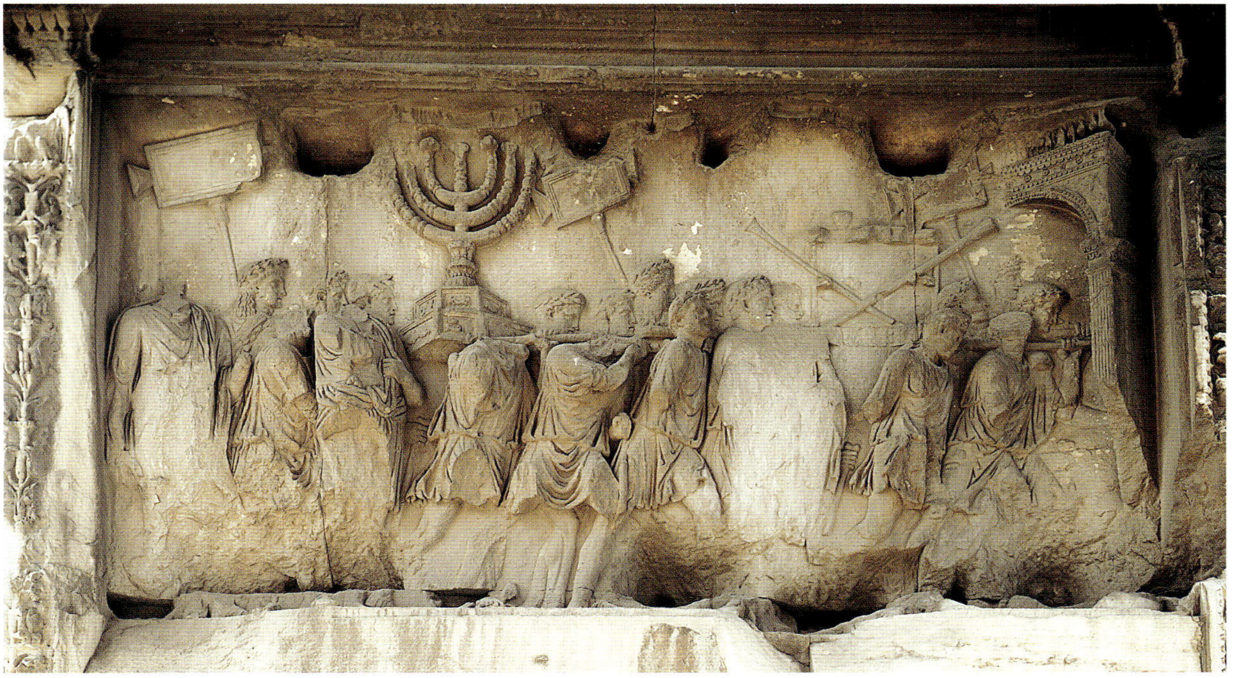

interesting for Mantegna being sculptural reliefs: those on the Arch of Trajan at Benevento in southern Italy (fig. 4) and, in Rome, those on the inner facades of the Arch of Titus (fig. 5) and on Trajan's column, as well as the detached panel of the triumph of Marcus Aurelius now in the Palazzo dei Conservatori but then on the Arch of Constantine. The artist supplemented these with innumerable details of armour, weapons and military paraphernalia, matching up terms found in the ancient sources with images from Roman remains, or his own imagination.[23]

Translating this reference material into a coherent and moving narrative was a huge challenge to Mantegna's powers of invention and design. From what must have been a lengthy and elaborate process of preparation there remains a handful of drawings and engravings apparently copied from his preliminary designs (see figs 2, 3, 6 and 7). They all have remarkably similar dimensions, at a scale of roughly 1:10 to the finished canvases, and it seems likely that they reflect demonstration drawings prepared both for the patron's approval and also for insertion into a mock-up of the whole ensemble. The inclusion of framing pilasters on a drawing for Canvas 1, in the Louvre, supports this conclusion (fig. 2).[24] In the canvases as painted, Mantegna made major changes from the earlier designs recorded in drawings and prints, simplifying and strengthening the compositions, enlarging and individualising the figures, and at times moving them from one canvas to another or changing them altogether. Importantly he also adopted a more strongly *di sotto in su* (upwards from below) perspectival viewpoint, increasing both the depth and the drama of the scenes.[25]

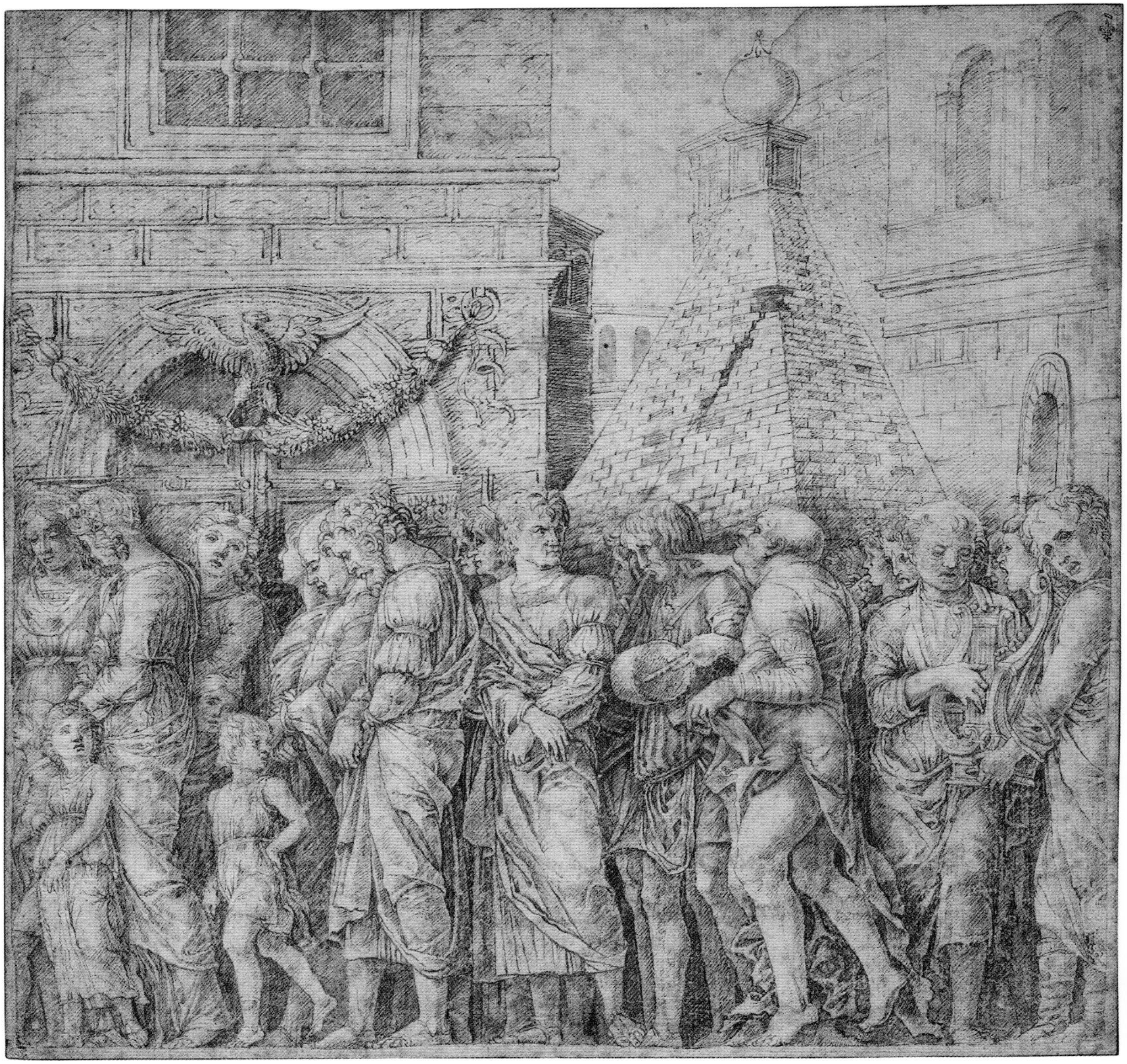

6 After Mantegna
Copy of preliminary study for Canvas 7,
The Captives, late fifteenth century
Pen and brown ink on paper, 27 × 27 cm
Musée Condé, Chantilly

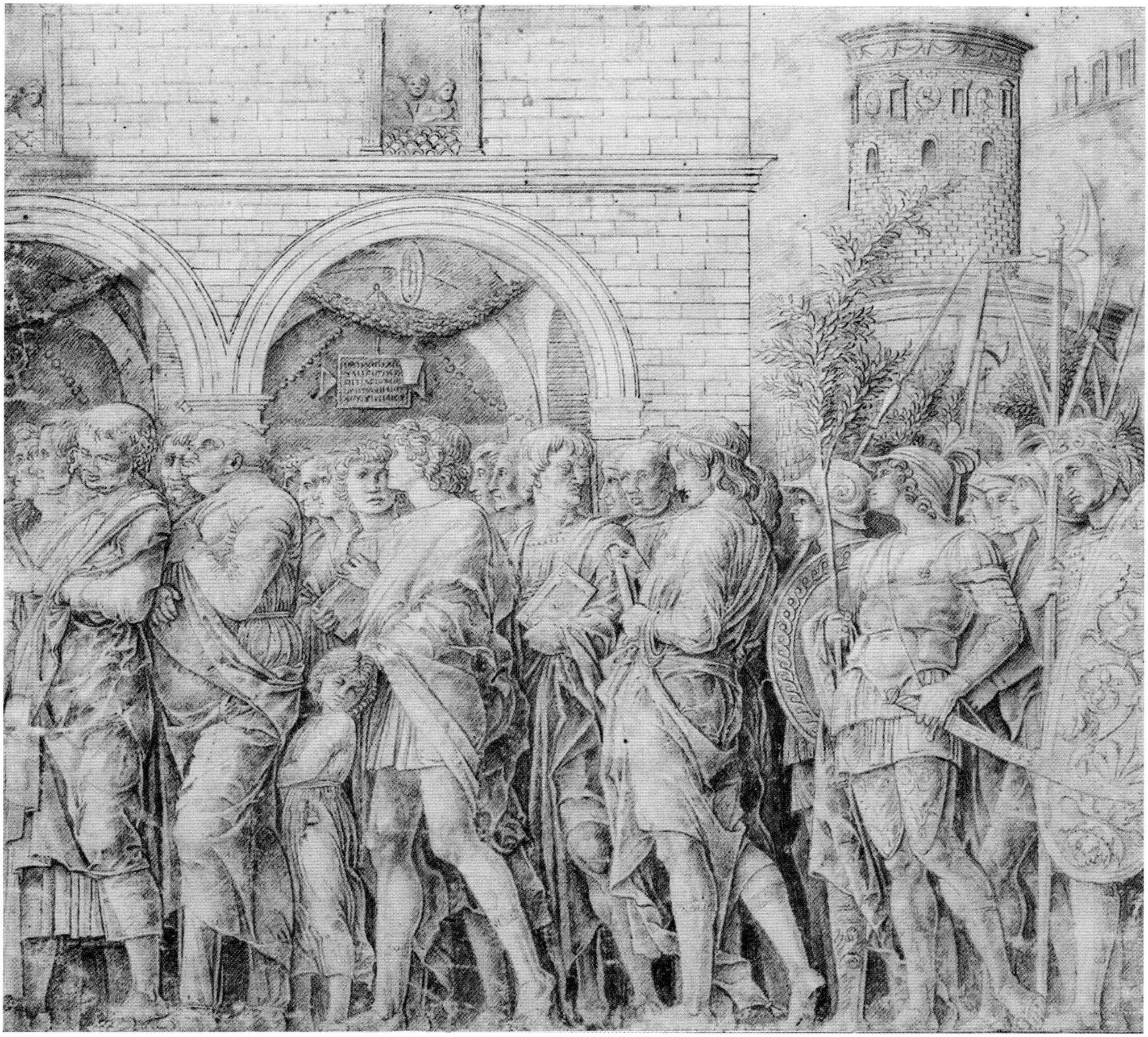

7 After Mantegna
Copy of preliminary study for *The Senators*
(not finally included), late fifteenth century
Pen and brown ink on paper, 28.9 × 26.8 cm
The Albertina Museum, Vienna

8 Detail of Canvas 4, *The Vase Bearers*, showing the vari-coloured marble vase

Beneath the now battered and restored paint surfaces of the canvases are exquisitely assured autograph underdrawings with occasional pentimenti (changes of mind), revealed by infrared reflectography.[26] Despite their ruined state, in many areas of the canvases it is still possible to see the minuteness and delicacy of Mantegna's handling of paint, the modelling carried out with the finest parallel hatching. It now seems extraordinary to us that the artist was able to paint such enormous canvases and achieve his colouristic effects without using oil, instead suspending his pigments in a less manipulable glue or egg tempera medium.[27]

The work on the *Triumphs* was interrupted by a long interval of time, 1488–90, that Mantegna spent away from Mantua painting Pope Innocent VIII's chapel at the Belvedere villa on the Vatican hill.[28] But the stay in Rome, which one might have expected to be decisive for this most antiquarian of artists, seems not to have significantly changed his approach to antiquity in general or the challenges of the *Triumphs* in particular. It used to be thought that he painted the canvases in processional order from left to right, and that the whole series was completed by 1494 when the Florentine Giovanni di Pierfrancesco de' Medici was taken to see 'the triumphs'.[29] Andrew Martindale thought that the last three scenes – the *Captives*, *Standard Bearers* and *Caesar on his Chariot*, and especially Canvas 7, the *Captives* – were the only ones to show a direct response to the Roman urban fabric.[30] But several writers have objected, pointing out that the street scene in the *Captives* is not particularly Roman, while its prominent pilaster capital comes from a Veronese antiquity, the Porta dei Leoni. Charles Hope has argued instead that Mantegna began with the right-hand group of three canvases, including the culminating signature scene of the Triumphator on his chariot, and reached a peak of mastery and confidence in the middle triplet, Canvases 4 to 6, which according to this hypothesis would have been the last to be painted. Six of the canvases could then date from after the Roman visit, and Mantegna could have continued to work on the series for the rest of his life.[31] The hypothesis cannot be proved or refuted on documentary or stylistic grounds, especially given the varying state of conservation of the canvases. What can be agreed is that the stylistic points of comparison for most of the *Triumphs* within Mantegna's oeuvre link them to works that can be dated from the mid-1490s to 1506, especially to the *Introduction of the Cult of Cybele at Rome* now in the National Gallery (see fig. 16, p. 27, left in the artist's studio at his death in 1506), which shares the *Triumphs*' powerful sense of movement and drama.[32] It was in that year that preparations were actively under way for the installation of the *Triumphs* in the Palazzo di San Sebastiano, when framing pilasters were commissioned from woodworkers in Venice.[33]

It is worth pausing to focus on Canvas 4, *The Vase Bearers*, which remains the most visually compelling of the series for its combination of overall legibility with extensive areas of original paint, as is confirmed by infrared reflectography that shows the confidence and quality of Mantegna's underdrawing. For example,

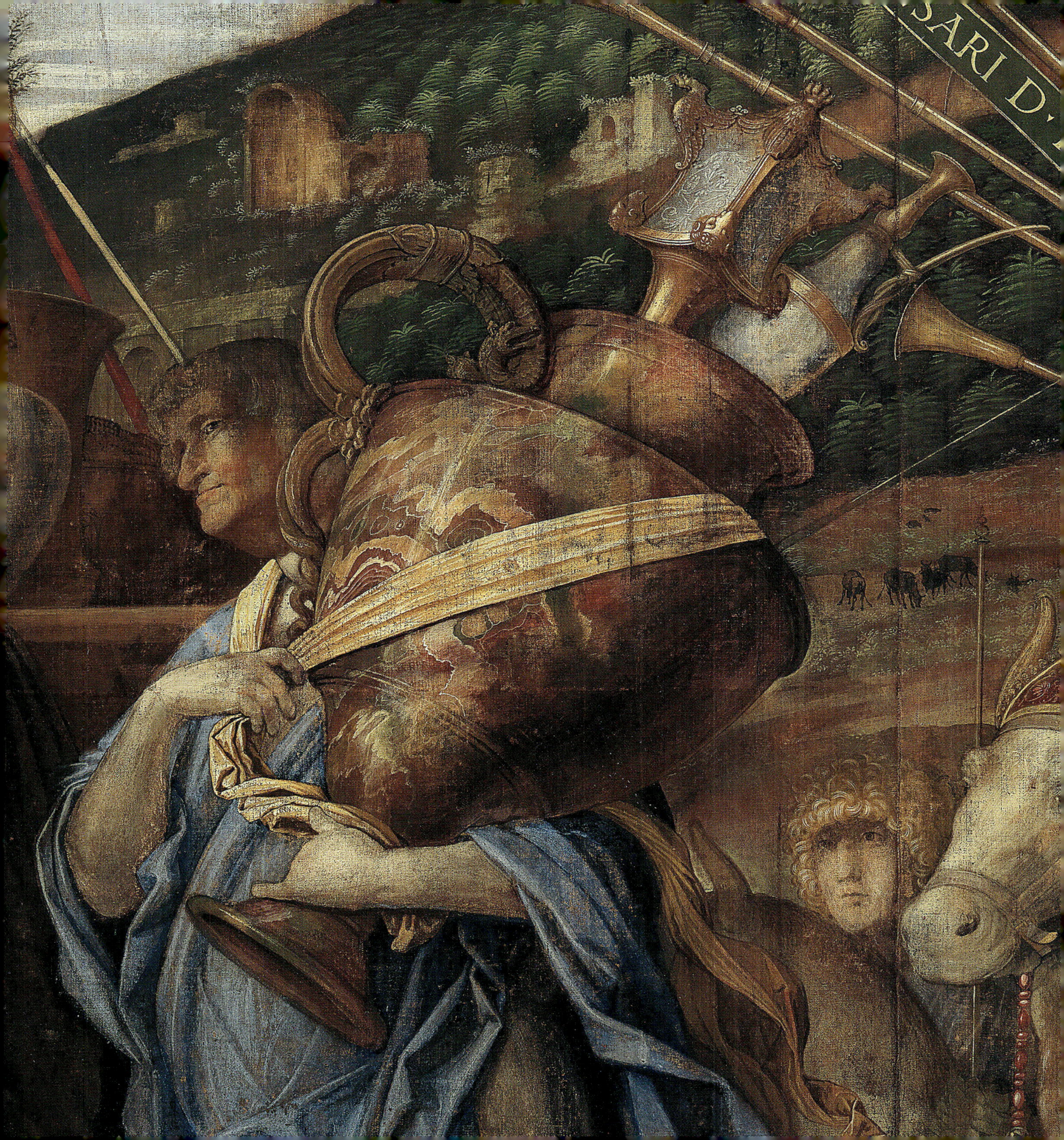
SARI D·

9 Detail of Canvas 4, *The Vase Bearers*, showing the blond young man

beautiful and accurate underdrawing is visible beneath the clumsily repainted left hand of the vase-bearer in blue. The canvas depicts bearers of booty and vases, trumpeters and sacrificial oxen led by youths, in the middle section of Caesar's triumphal procession. The main literary source for the items shown here – the metal vases at left so weightily packed with silver and gold coins that each had to be carried by four men, the trumpeters, the oxen with gilded horns, garlands and triangular head dresses (*mitrae*) led by boys in sashes holding bowls – was Plutarch's account of the Macedonian Triumph of Aemilius Paulus in 167 BC.[34] The vari-coloured marble vase given pride of place (fig. 8), its handle composed of two gold scaly serpents bound together, is so precisely rendered that the image could be given to a craftsman for manufacture in three dimensions; it is a manifestation of Mantegna's obsession with observed materiality,[35] as are the other vessels, rendered with equally loving precision.

The brilliant composition has a masterly sense of swinging movement seen from below. Behind the processional figures there rises the smooth curved silhouette of a hill studded and capped with highly impressive but partially ruined ancient buildings (the painting here is very well preserved). Halfway down the wooded slopes is a stretch of pasture with a central group of ruminating cows, while to the right a shepherd leans on his stick to gaze across the valley at the procession, his sheep lowering their necks to graze obliviously around him. Although the buildings are not in any sense copies of actual antiquities, Mantegna was surely drawing on the experience of seeing vaulted imperial ruins against hillsides in Rome, for example on the Palatine. Particularly happy inventions are the round three-storied and arcaded building with its Colosseum-like articulation and the giant column with fluted shaft and composite capital bearing a colossal statue with arm upraised as if in salutation to the triumphal procession.

Perhaps the most beautiful figure of the whole series of canvases is the youth with blond ringlets at the right, his upraised arm rendered like porcelain (fig. 9). The ribbon-like reins of the ox are wound twice around his thumb and then held with such delicacy between thumb and forefingers that one is tempted to see him as carrying out some ceremonial lustration of the sacrificial beast.

The *Triumphs* have always been best known by reputation and at second hand, through various types of copy and reproduction, some produced very early on. Two copper plates engraved back and front with *Triumphs* scenes were listed in Ludovico Mantegna's post-mortem inventory of 1510, only four years after his father's death.[36] The retention of the plates demonstrates that these engravings were produced within the workshop, and presumably at Mantegna's own initiative, though not executed by his own hand. They include scenes identifiable as corresponding to those in Canvases 5 and 6 (the *Elephants*, fig. 10, and the *Corselet Bearers*) but reproducing preliminary drawings, as discussed earlier, rather than the finished canvases. Another scene known from both workshop

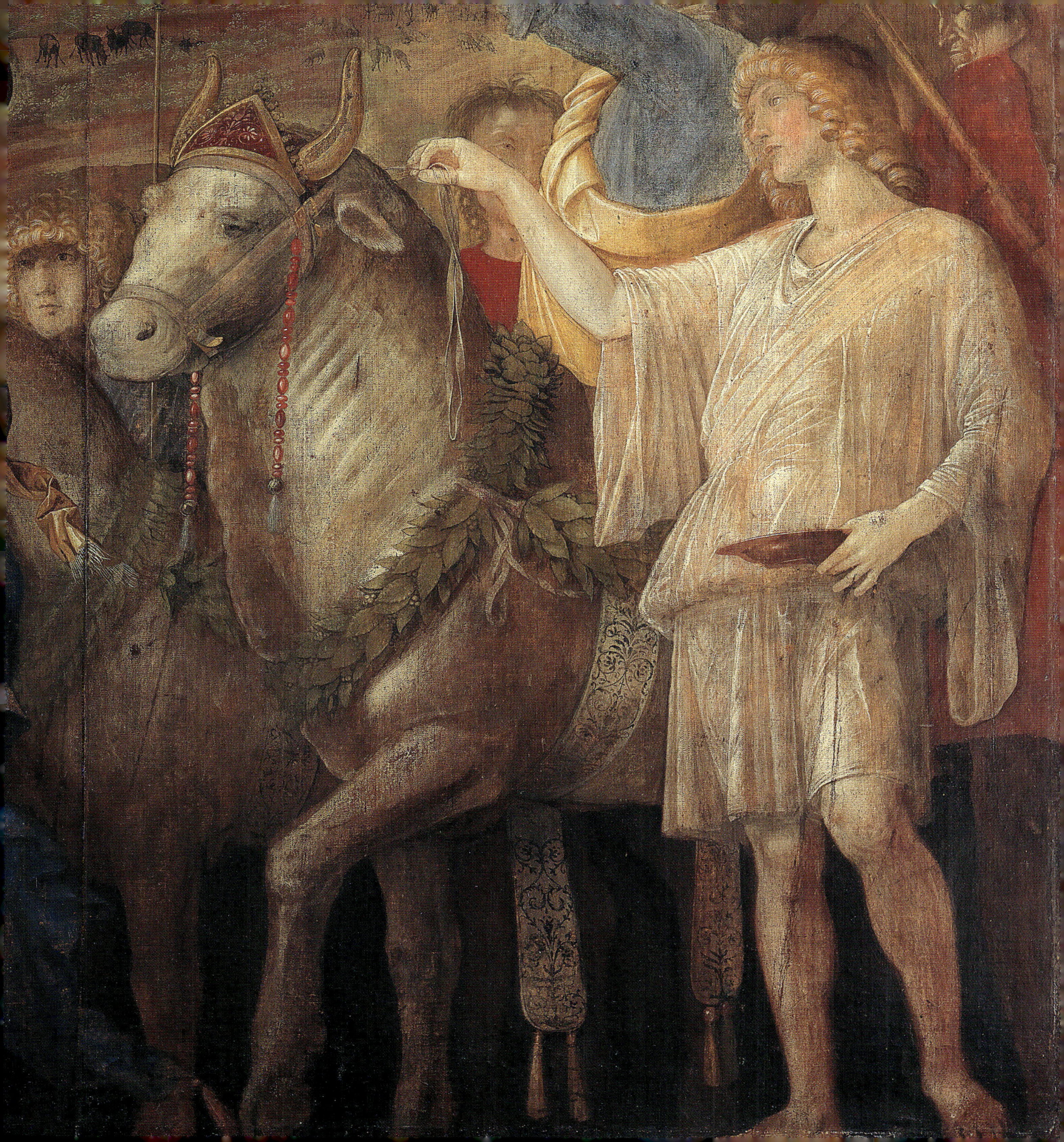

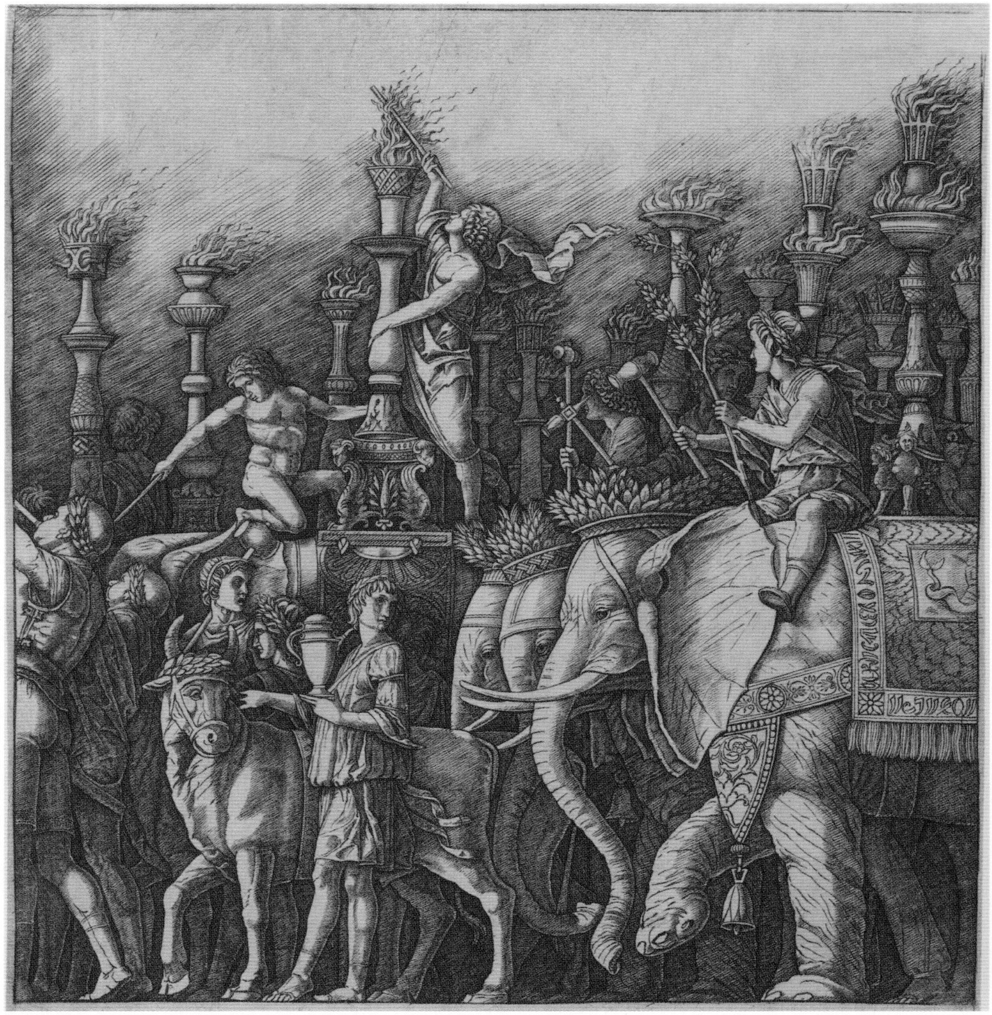

LEFT:

10 Workshop of Mantegna, attributed to Giulio Campagnola (about 1482–1515/18)
The Elephants, around 1497
Engraving, 28.2 × 26.8 cm
The Metropolitan Museum of Art, New York. Bequest of Phyllis Massar, 2011

OPPOSITE:

11 Niccolò Giolfino (about 1476–1555); formerly attributed to Liberale da Verona (about 1445–1527/9)
Dido's Suicide, early sixteenth century
Oil on poplar, 42.5 × 123.2 cm
The National Gallery, London

drawing and engraving (usually known as the *Senators*, see fig. 7) does not appear in the final sequence of canvases. The similarity of its composition to that of the *Captives* suggests that it was purposely omitted.

Through these workshop prints, and copies of them by Giovanni Antonio da Brescia, the *Triumphs* influenced artists north and south of the Alps in the early sixteenth century.[37] An early example from the nearby city of Verona is an attractive panel from a cassone front depicting *Dido's Suicide*, fortuitously now in the National Gallery, London (fig. 11) where the painter, probably Niccolò Giolfino (about 1476–1555), used figures and details from the *Senators* and the *Corselet Bearers* engravings.[38]

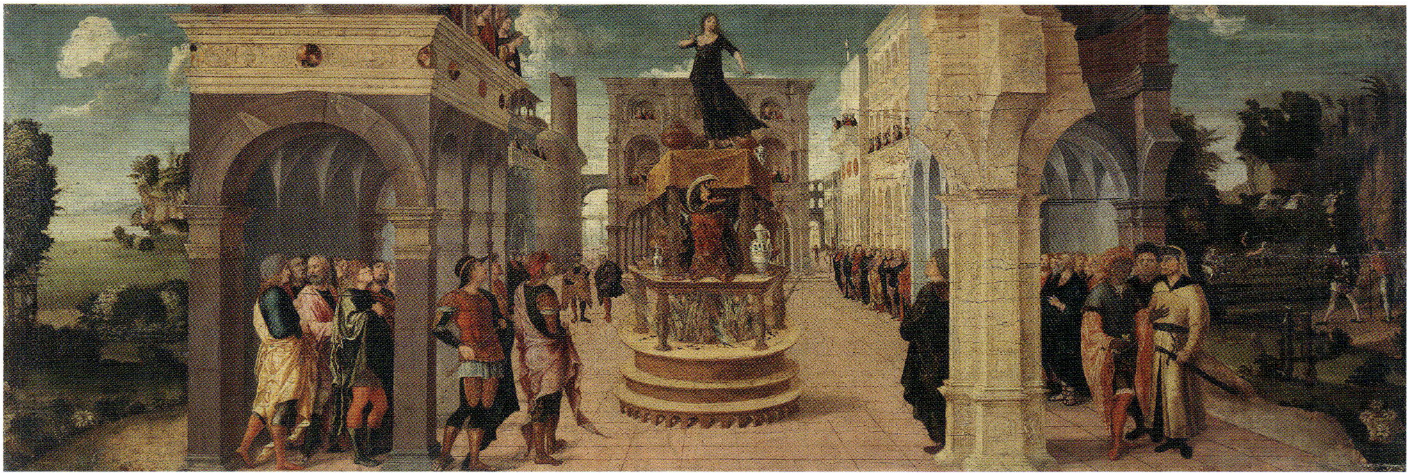

It is beyond the scope of this essay to trace the fortunes of the *Triumphs* through the great tradition of European art, from Giulio Romano to Edgar Degas, but one name has to be mentioned: that of Peter Paul Rubens, the most competitively voracious of all Mantegna's admirers. His *Roman Triumph* in the National Gallery in London (fig. 12) is characteristically cannibalistic, to brilliant effect. Rubens, who had worked in Mantua in 1600–8, owned small-scale copies of at least five of the *Triumphs* canvases, probably commissioned by himself. Three of them are in Prague and are all reworked to a greater or lesser extent, perhaps by his pupil Erasmus Quellinus.[39] Two more were physically incorporated into the National Gallery picture and reworked by Rubens himself. He took the complete copy of the *Elephants* and the right-hand section of the *Vase Bearers*, stitched them together with a third canvas including figures inspired by the *Captives*, and then painted over the whole composition, adding the dancing girls on the left, making the elephants more ferocious and zoologically correct, and inserting larger, more archaeologically observed ruins on the hillside.[40]

Rubens could draw not only on his own copies and memories of the original canvases, but also on Andrea Andreani's woodcuts of the triumphs of 1598–9, the first reproductions of the entire series (fig. 13). If it is hard for a modern eye, avid for the magic of originality, to derive much excitement from Andreani's renderings, this was certainly not the case in earlier centuries. It was on Andreani, and on the workshop engravings, that Goethe relied to write what is perhaps the most searching analysis ever produced of Mantegna's achievement.[41] At first viewing, Goethe writes, there seems a contradiction between the artist's strenuous search for an ideal, classicising style and his desire to convey the particularity and the naturalness of a teeming variety of human (and animal) figures. The high and the ideal are manifest, but 'nature also forces her way in with a primitive violence', so that 'the study of the Antique provides the form, but nature the skill, and in the end, the life'.[42] For Goethe these two elements remained finally irreconcilable, since Mantegna was not a 'High Renaissance' artist: he 'was called upon to undertake this adventure at a time when a developing

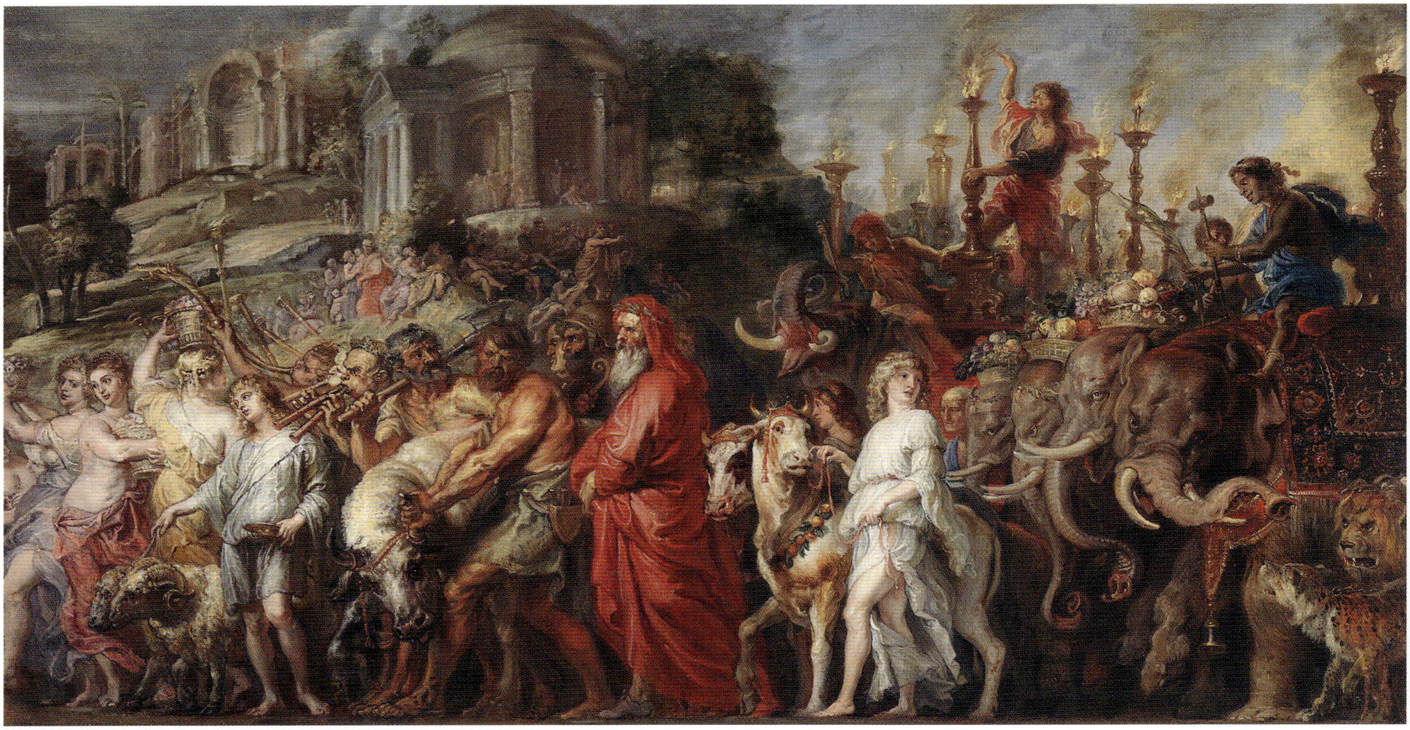

high art was not yet able to give a clear account of its aims and capacities'.[43] One might instead suggest that this unresolved contradiction between high ideal and natural particularity, between the form and the life, is what gives Mantegna's *Triumphs* their special edge to an audience more attuned to the qualities of early Italian art.

The *Triumphs* encompass the whole spectrum of Mantegna's expressive range, from crabbiness to exaltation, from tragic grimness to delicious humour. We see the paranoia that recurs in other works and in his correspondence in the inscription referring to the overcoming of envy (*invidia*).[44] We feel the heroic grandeur of ancient Rome in all its relentless triumphalism and what Roger Fry called 'a change from a dramatic to an epic presentment' in Mantegna's style.[45] We are witnesses to a joyous festive quality tinged with melancholy; a sense of the transitory nature of empire conveyed in the already ruined buildings on the hillside; a sympathy for animals and children unconscious of their eventual fate. We come away, our heads swimming with images: trumpeters with distended cheeks, tragic rows of captives, the empty corselets of defeated warriors, but also prancing children, dishevelled dogs, ringleted horses, elephants with earrings, and even a pair of scissors and a spoon dangling from a litter (in Canvas 3).[46]

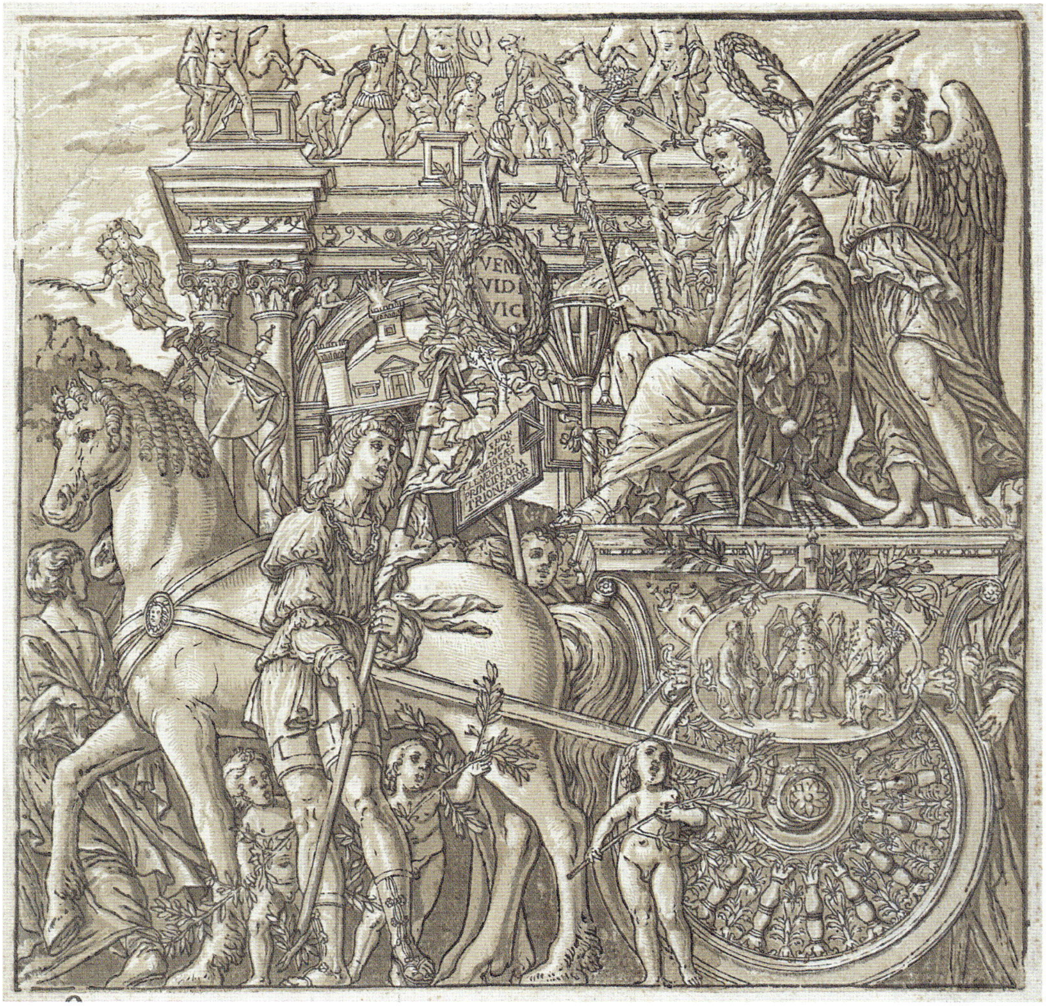

OPPOSITE:

12 Peter Paul Rubens (1577–1640)
Roman Triumph, about 1630
Oil on canvas, mounted on wood, 86.8 × 163.9 cm
The National Gallery, London

ABOVE:

13 Andrea Andreani (1558/9–1629), after Mantegna
Caesar in his Horse-Drawn Chariot,
Sheet 9 from *The Triumph of Julius Caesar*, 1598–9
Chiaroscuro woodcut, one of 10 sheets, 37 × 37.5 cm
The Metropolitan Museum of Art, New York
Rogers Fund, 1922 (22.73.3-97)

THE TRIUMPHS OF CAESAR

1. THE TRUMPETERS

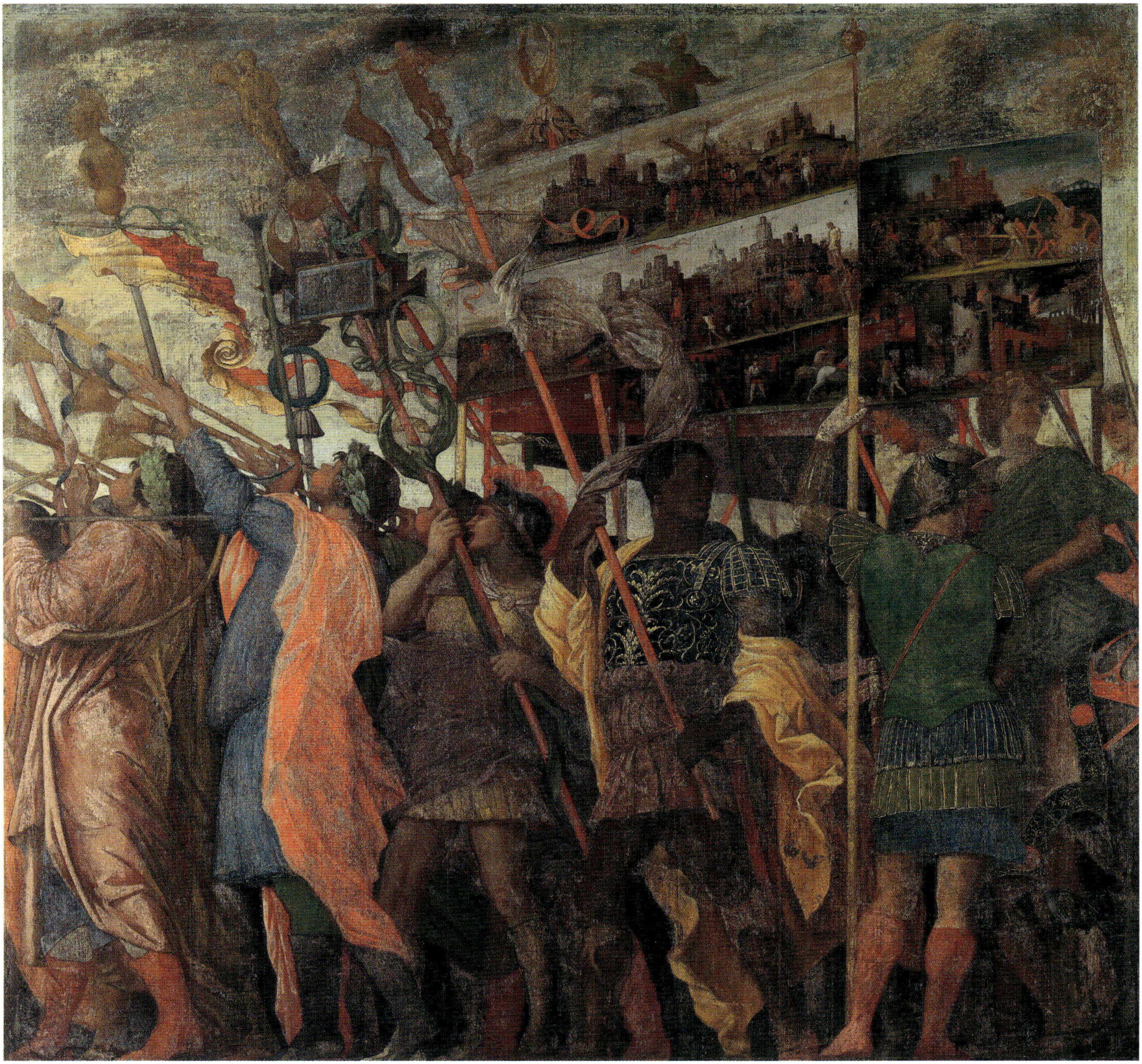

2. THE TRIUMPHAL CARTS

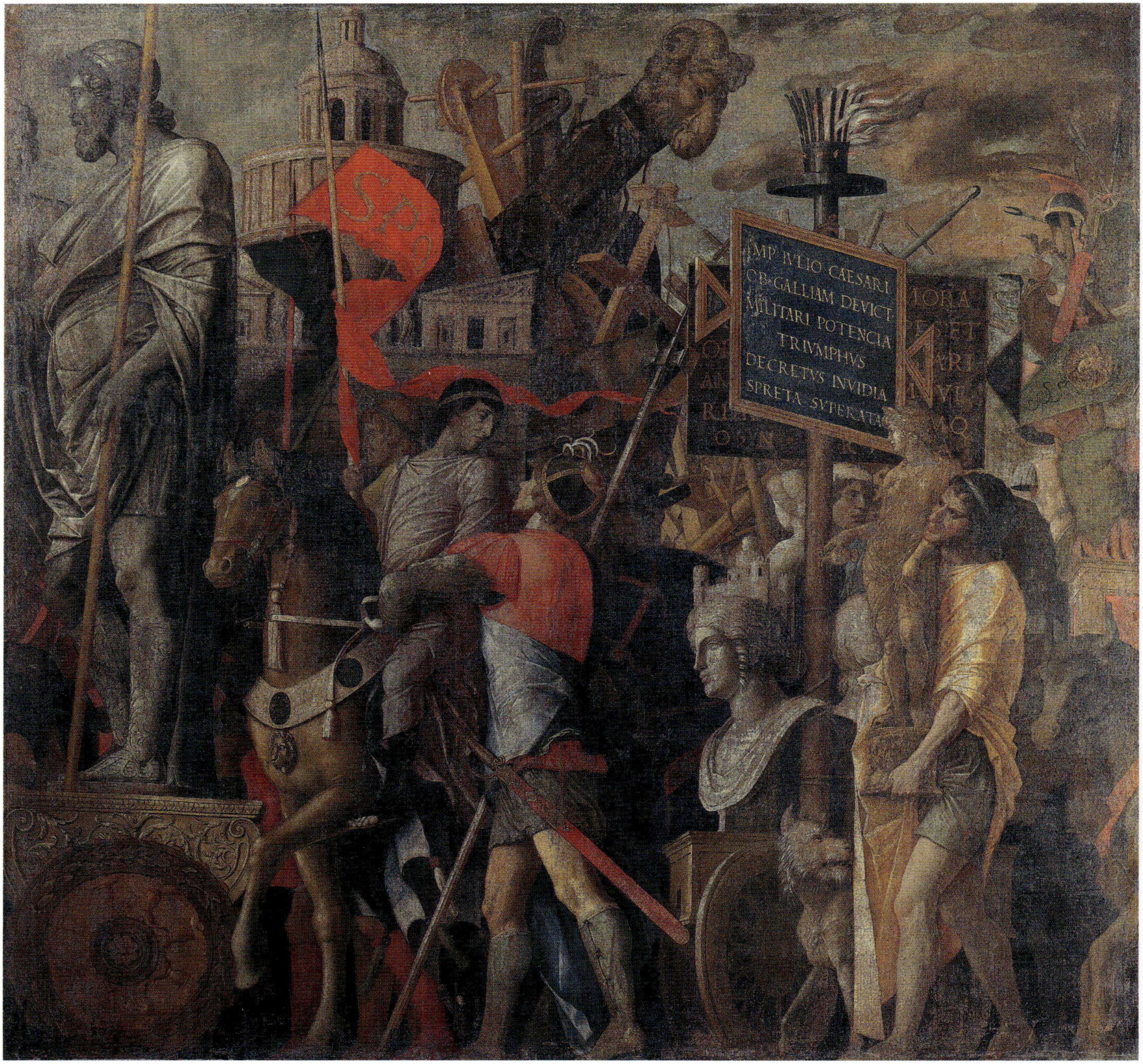

3. THE TROPHY BEARERS

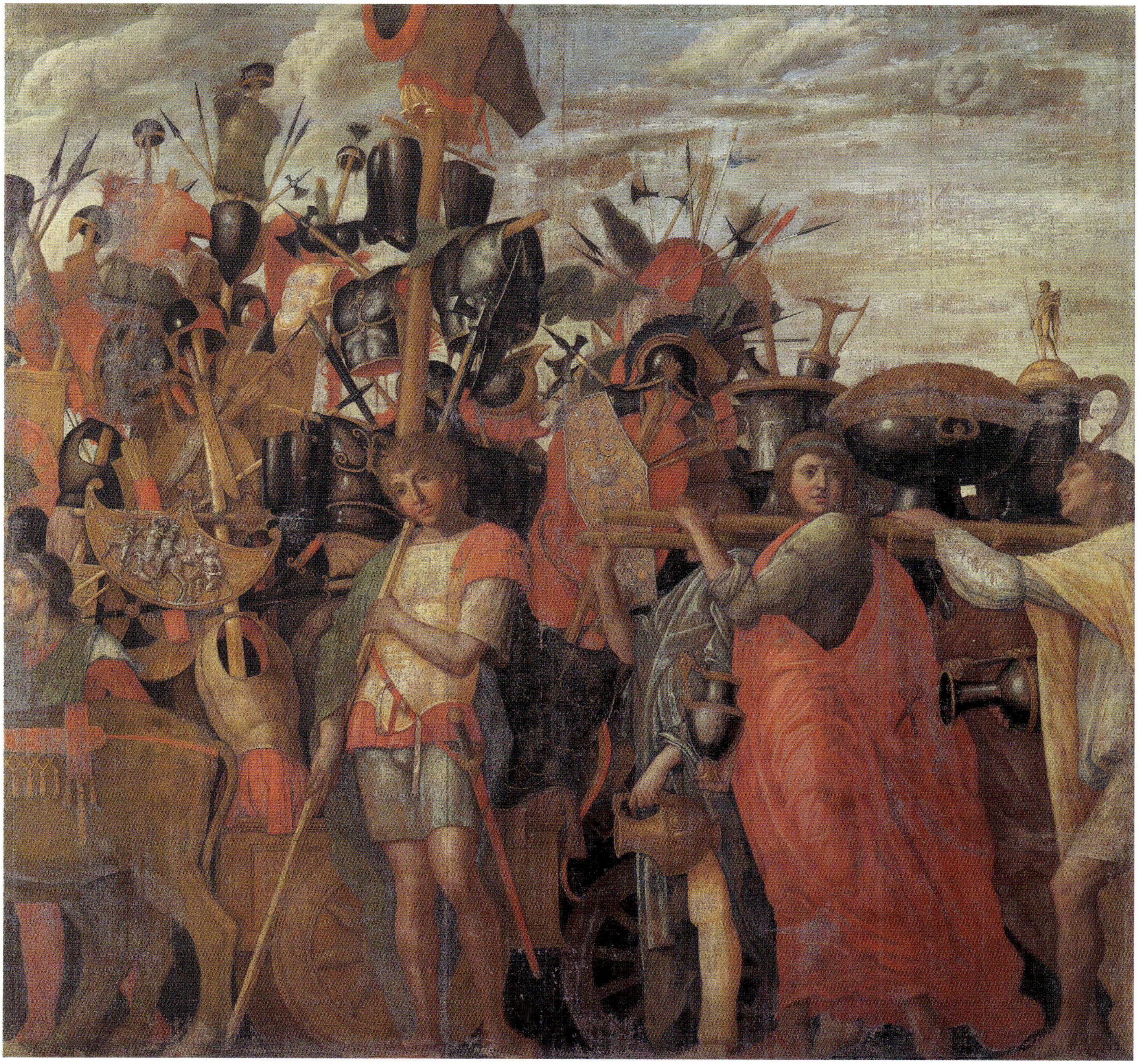

4. THE VASE BEARERS

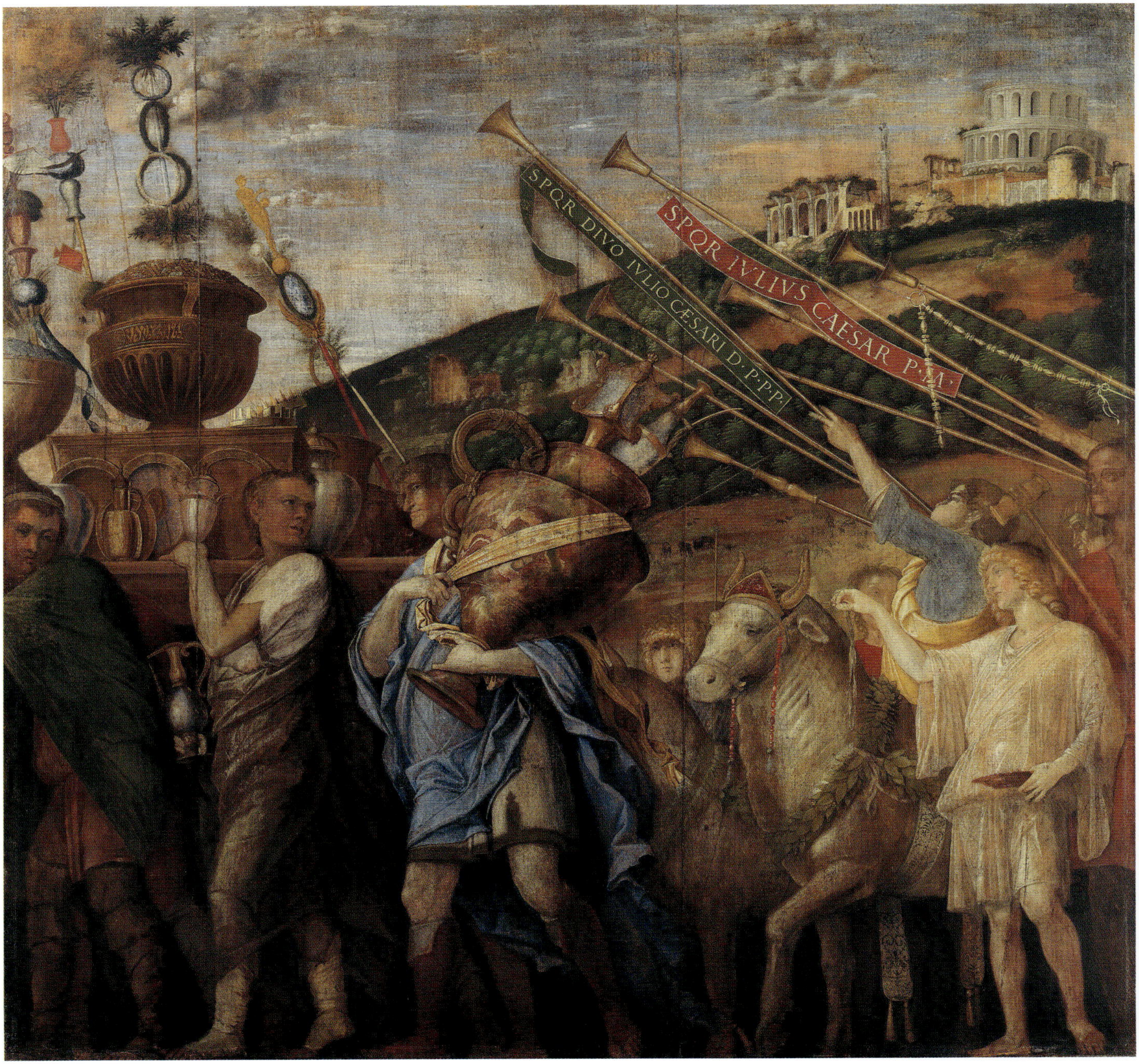

5. THE ELEPHANTS

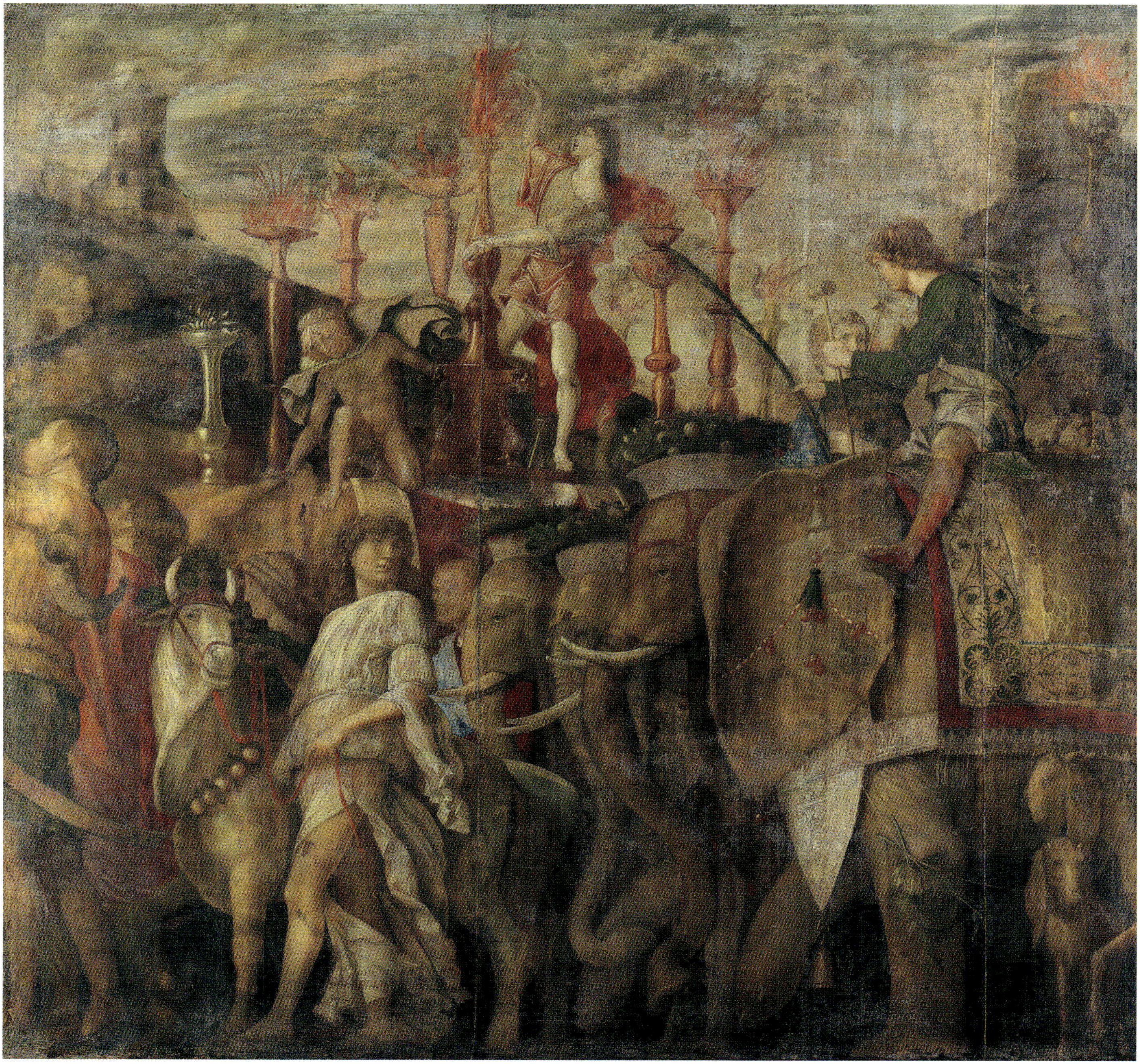

6. THE CORSELET BEARERS

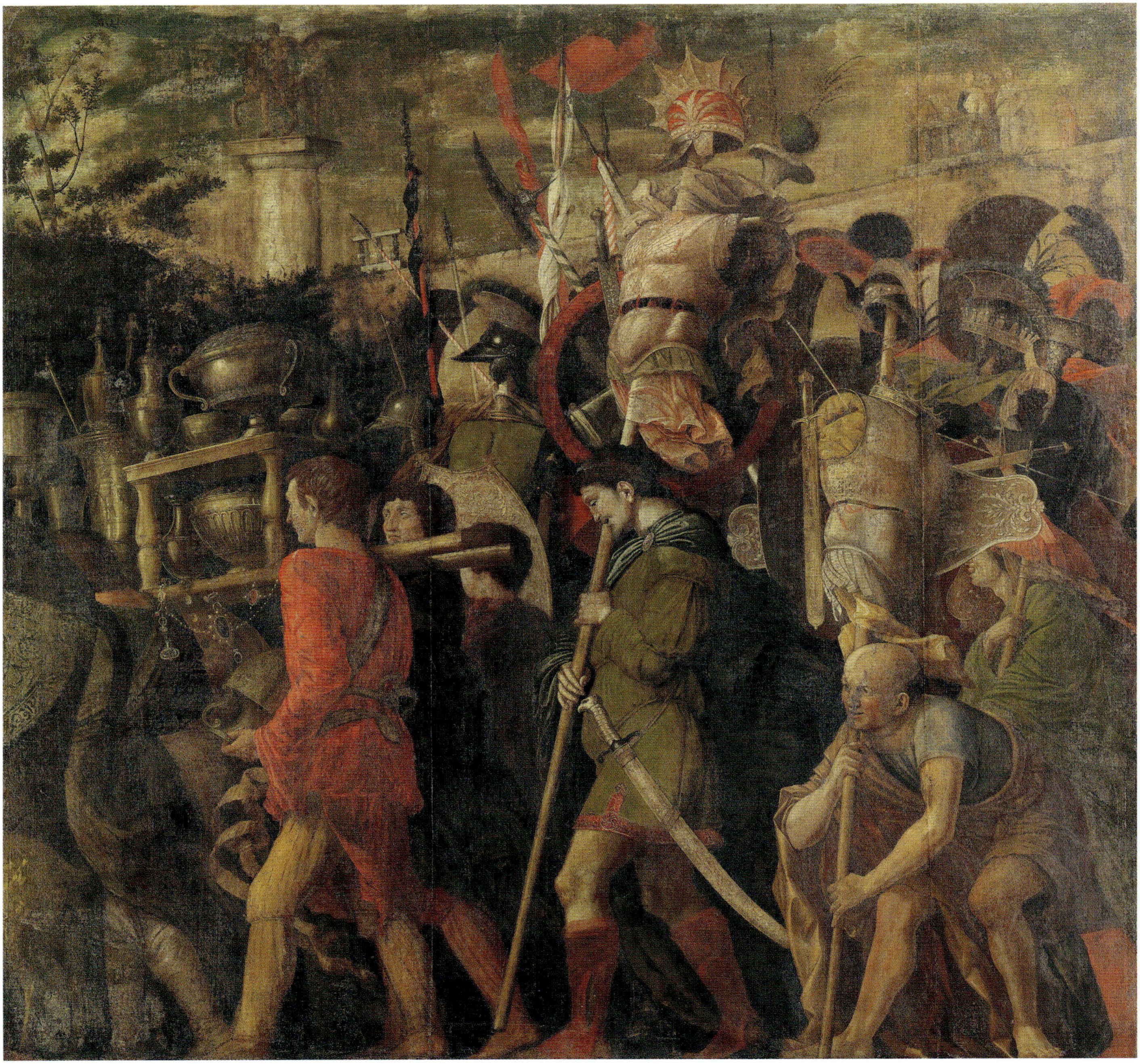

7. THE CAPTIVES

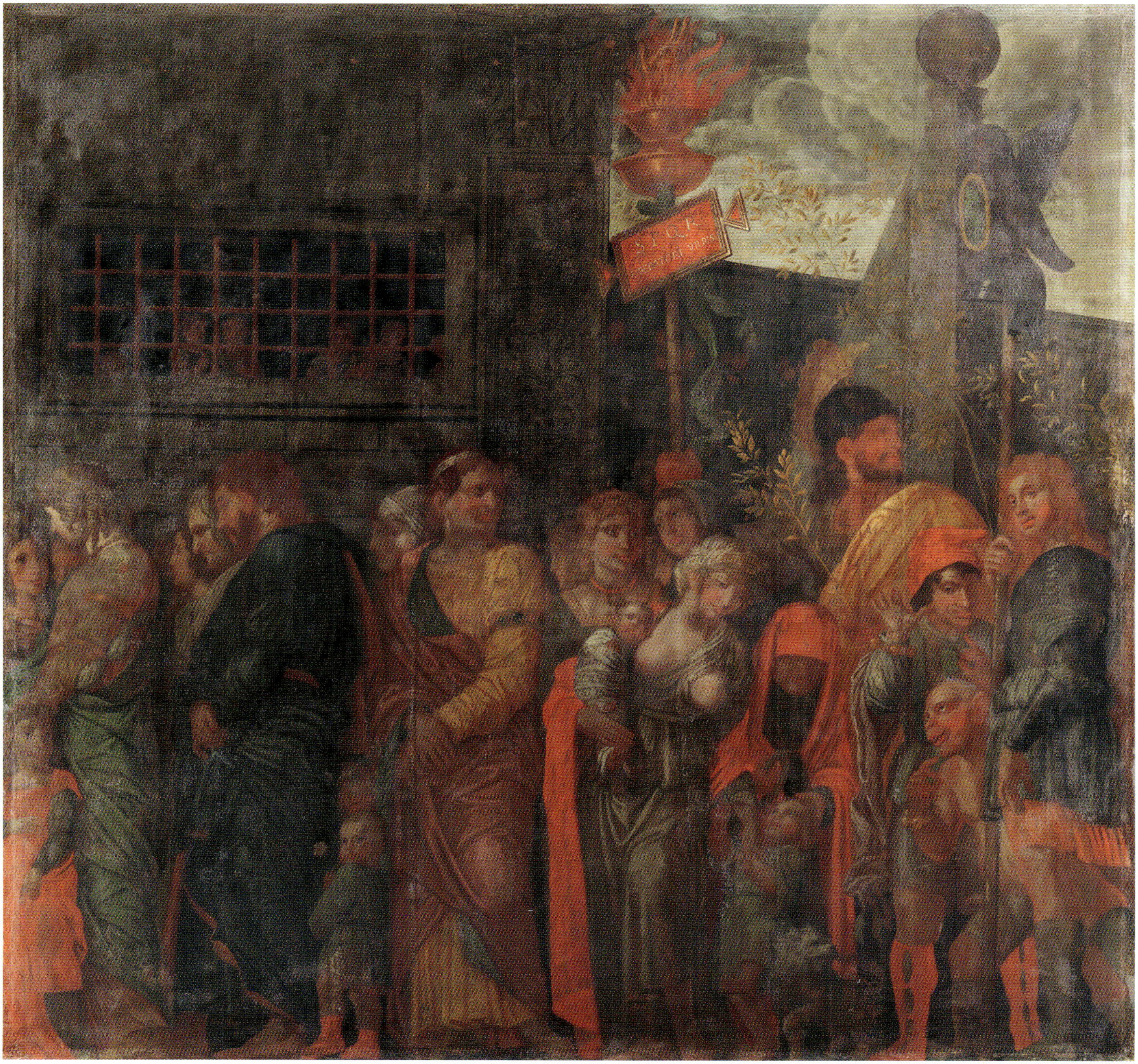

8. THE MUSICIANS

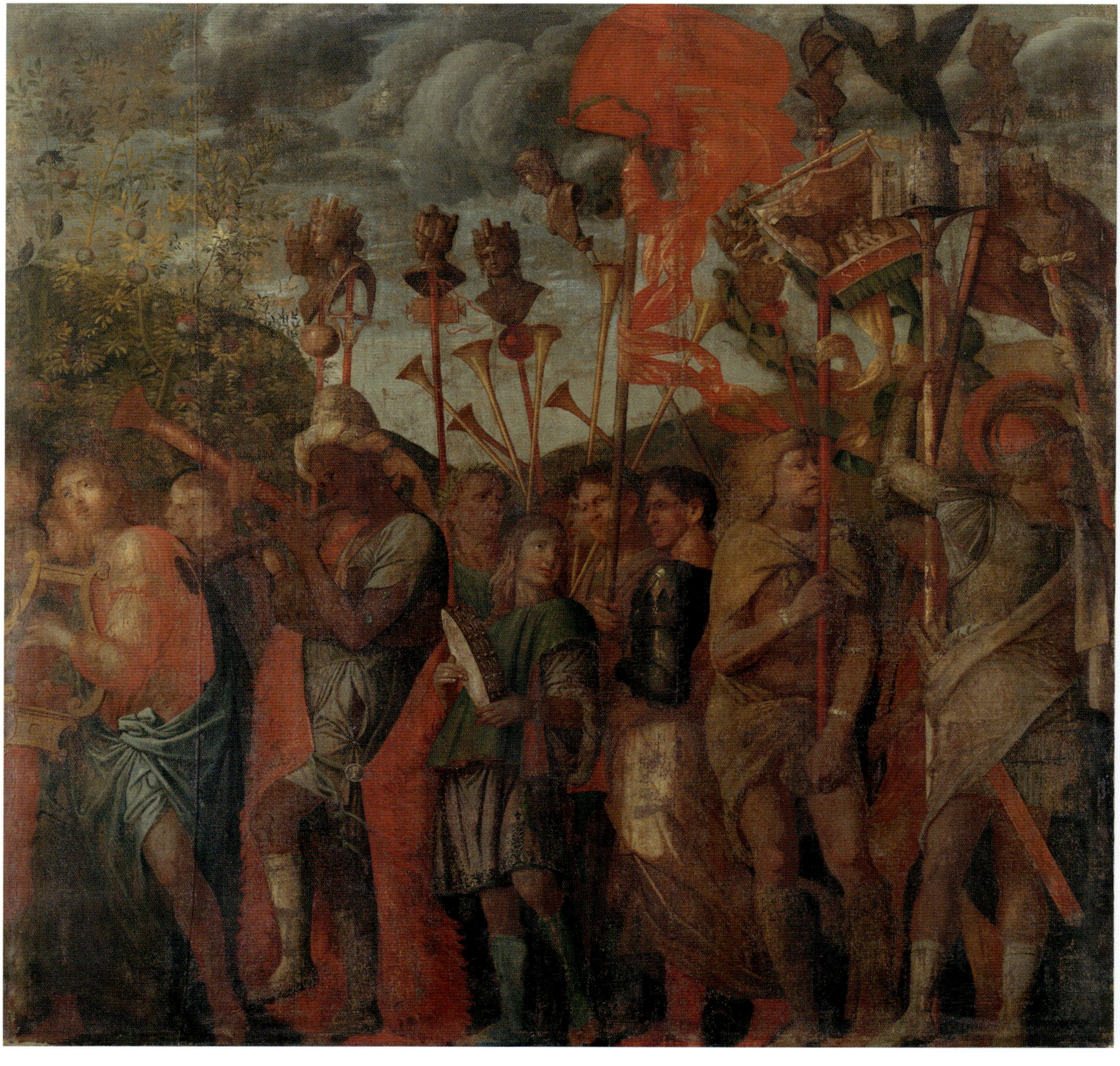

9. CAESAR ON HIS CHARIOT

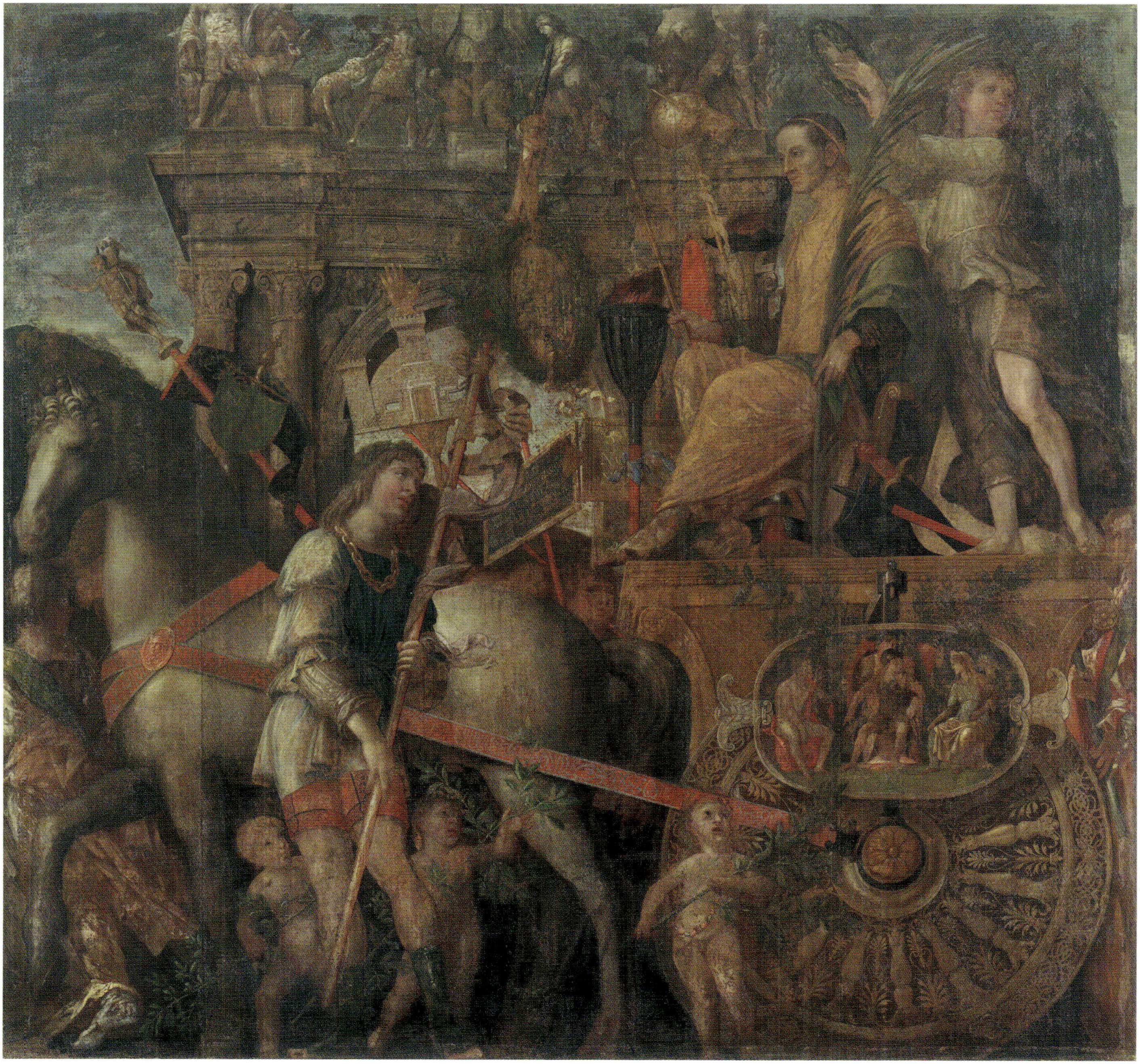

NOTES

Andrea Mantegna: Court Artist to the Gonzaga of Mantua

GUIDO REBECCHINI

1. Kristeller 1901, p. 467. On Mantegna and the Gonzaga, see Lightbown 1986, pp. 81–97.
2. Lightbown 1986, pp. 30–46; N. Rowley, '"Sculpting in paint": Mantegna's Training in Padua', in London and Berlin 2018–19, pp. 89–93.
3. C. Campbell in London and Berlin 2018–19, pp. 135–9.
4. For more detailed discussion of the relationship between the two artists, see London and Berlin 2018–19.
5. Di Monte 2007.
6. Lightbown 1986, pp. 59–80.
7. Agosti 2005, p. 30 and Ames-Lewis, pp. 127–8.
8. Lightbown 1986, pp. 412–15.
9. L. Attardi in Paris 2008–9, pp. 188–93.
10. Lightbown 1986, pp. 99–117; S. Bandera, 'Camera picta', in Turin 2019, pp. 102–9.
11. Tavernor 1998, pp. 159–88.
12. Signorini 1996.
13. Canova 2001.
14. Elam in London 1981, p. 15.
15. See Thiébaut in Paris 2008–9, n. 76, pp. 221–3 and Lightbown 1986, n. 23, pp. 421–3, respectively.
16. Alberti 2004, p. 65.
17. Ames-Lewis 2000, p. 76.
18. Fusco and Corti 2006, p. 148.
19. Bourne 2008, pp. 72–86.
20. Lightbown 1986, cat. 32, pp. 436–7 and cat. 49, pp. 448–9, respectively.
21. For a biography of Isabella d'Este, see Shaw 2019.
22. Campbell 2004a.
23. Brown 2002.
24. Lightbown 1986, pp. 224–5.
25. London and Berlin 2018–19.
26. Blumenröder 2008.
27. Lightbown 1986, pp. 214–18.
28. London 2002, cat. 37, pp. 107–8.
29. Ames-Lewis 2000, pp. 102–5.
30. Ekserdjian 1997, pp. 24–5.
31. Rebecchini 2021.
32. Rebecchini 2019, p. 184.

Mantegna's Triumphs: Form and Life

CAROLINE ELAM

Appendix

Conservation history of the Triumphs

Having been acquired by Charles I in 1629–30 and installed at Hampton Court Palace, the *Triumphs*, already flaking badly, were treated by restorers in three campaigns in the late seventeenth and early eighteenth century: three canvases were worked on by Parry Walton by 1693, the whole series was completely repainted by Louis Laguerre by 1702 and more work was done by Joseph Goupy in 1717 (Martindale 1979, ch. 10). In 1910–21 Roger Fry, with various friends including Edward Wadsworth, worked on Canvas 1, doing much repainting in tempera, including the face of the Black standard bearer (since reconstructed by John Brealey). In 1930–4 Kennedy North carried out a relining of all the canvases with copious quantities of wax (Martindale 1979, ch. 11, and Royal Collection files). From 1962 to 1974 John Brealey and Joan Seddon worked on all but Canvas 7 (thought to be untreatable), removing as much of the wax and the old repaints as could safely be attempted (see Sir Anthony Blunt's introduction to Martindale 1979; no detailed report was ever produced). Following the Royal Academy of Arts' Mantegna exhibition in 1992 and the discovery in the Palazzo Ducale in Mantua of early sixteenth-century pilasters possibly originating from the room of the *Triumphs* at the Palazzo di San Sebastiano (Berzaghi 1990 and Agosti 1992), the *Triumphs* were redisplayed at Hampton Court in a continuous series divided by framing pilasters copied from those in Mantua. Canvas 7, the *Captives*, was reintegrated into the series following minor treatment in 1995 by Rupert Featherstone who did not attempt to remove Kennedy North's relining or the Laguerre repaints.

1. Letter from Andrea Mantegna in Rome to Marquis Francesco Gonzaga in Mantua, 31 January 1489; Kristeller 1902, doc. 102.
2. Vasari 1966–87, Testo III, p. 551: 'è la miglior cosa che lavorasse mai'. For the critical fortunes of the *Triumphs* up to the 1630s, see Agosti 2005. The fundamental study of the *Triumphs* remains Martindale 1979, with important new hypotheses in Hope 1985, re-presented by him in London and New York 1992, pp. 350–71, and re-stated by him with further argumentation in Mantua 2006b, pp. 287–97. A thorough discussion in Lightbown 1986, ch. 8, pp. 140–54, and acute observations in S. J. Campbell, 'Mantegna's Triumph: The Cultural Politics of Imitation "all'antica" at the Court of Mantua, 1490–1530', in Campbell 2004b, pp. 91–105; and in Campbell 2020, pp. 254–72. Most recently, see V. Farinella 'I trionfi (e i lamenti) di Cesare', in Turin 2019, pp. 144–51.
3. See Beard 2007. Beard points out that the ancient descriptions of triumphs are themselves historical constructions, a useful comment when assessing Mantegna's 'anachronisms'.
4. See Appendix.
5. B. Furlotti and G. Rebecchini, '"Rare and unique in this world": Mantegna's *Triumph* and the Gonzaga Collection', in London 2018, pp. 54–9.

6. Martindale 1979, ch. 3, proposed Ludovico Gonzaga as the initiating patron and the Corridoio del Passerino in the Corte Vecchia of the Palazzo Ducale, Mantua, as the intended location. Lack of acceptance of these particular conclusions by subsequent writers does not undermine the many indispensable elements in Martindale's book. Tosetti Grandi 2008 has reproposed Ludovico as patron.
7. Kristeller 1902, doc. 96. See Canova 2007, for the correction that the visiting 'Duca' was not, as usually assumed, Ercole d'Este of Ferrara, but rather the 14-year-old Guidobaldo da Montefeltro of Urbino.
8. Kristeller 1902, doc. 115. Francesco's patronage has been accepted by most writers since Kristeller.
9. Equicola 1521, book 4, cited in Martindale 1979, p. 185, doc. 26: 'In the furthest part of the city, near the church of San Sebastiano a most proud and beautiful palace, in order to install in one room, built solely for this purpose, the Triumph of Caius Julius Caesar, a labour of many years by Andrea Mantegna'. For the palace, later much altered, see Berzaghi 1990; Brown 1997. The canvases were hung in a single sequence.
10. As argued by D.S. Chambers, 'Il Marchese Federico Gonzaga (1441–1484) e il Trionfo di Cesare di Andrea Mantegna', in Signorini 2010, pp. 507–20, taking up a passing suggestion made by Elam in London 1981, p. 22.
11. See Hope in London and New York 1992, p. 356; Campbell 2004b, p. 95. Mantegna referred to them in 1489 as 'li trionfi mei'; Kristeller 1902, doc. 102. In reply (ibid., p. 81) Francesco expresses his desire to see them finished and adds: 'although it is the work of your hands and your genius, nonetheless we glory in having them in the house.'
12. Pinelli 1985; for a summary of the references to the *Triumphs of Petrarch*, see Brown in Mantua 2006, pp. 282–5.
13. See Ferino-Pagden 2001.
14. See Romano 1981, pp. 20–2; Pinelli 1985, p. 295; Richards 2000, pp. 58–61.
15. See Gaspare's single-leaf *Triumph of Titus and Vespasian* in the Louvre, collection Esmond de Rothschild, inv. 774 DR, reproduced in Paris 2008–9, p. 375 (entry by Gennaro Toscano). For a comprehensive assessment of triumphal imagery in fifteenth-century manuscript illumination before Mantegna's cycle, see Armstrong 2008. Another extremely relevant example by Gaspare is the illumination of the *Triumph of Caesar* in Rome, Biblioteca Casanatense MS 453, fol. 2v, discussed by Armstrong, ibid. The manuscript was exhibited in Mantua 2006a, pp. 252–3, but this page was not illustrated. Gaspare's visual vocabulary was informed by Mantegna's earlier works; see G. Toscano, 'Gaspare da Padova e la diffusione della miniatura "all'antica" da Roma a Napoli', in Padua 1999, pp. 525–31.
16. They were lent in 1488 to Ercole d'Este of Ferrara: see Brown and Delmarcel 1996, pp. 33–6; New York 2002, pp. 91–6.
17. Documentation for 'Triumphs' (not always necessarily those by Mantegna) used in festivities is in Martindale 1979, pp. 183–4. For discussion of Mantegna's use of canvas supports, see Lightbown 1986, p. 150; Christiansen in London and New York 1992, pp. 68–9.
18. Now hard to read on the canvas, but easily legible on copies such as Andrea Andreani's woodcut (fig. 13).
19. Vowles 2019, citing an unpublished essay by Mauro Lucco, who suggests the architectural model labelled in the drawing 'ALESAN...' represents the Pharos (lighthouse) at Alexandria, one of the seven wonders of the ancient world. The drawing was sold at Sotheby's, New York, 29 January 2020, lot 19, as a Mantegna autograph, with extensive catalogue notes by David Ekserdjian and Cristiana Romalli.
20. The principal sources are Suetonius, *Vitae duodecim Caesarum*, Julius Caesar, 37–38 and Appian, *Romaica*, *Civil Wars*, book II, ch. XV, paras 101–2.
21. Marcanova's lost work of around 1460 is referred to in his *Collectio antiquitatum*, fol. 4, as 'our book which we have composed concerning the dignities of Roman triumphs and military matters'. For Biondo and Mantua see Tosetti Grandi 2008 and M.A. Pincelli, 'La *Roma triumphans* e la nascita dell'antiquario Biondo Flavio e Andrea Mantegna', in Calvano et al. 2010, pp. 79–98. Another less important contemporary source, which may have furnished some details, was Roberto Valturio's *De Re Militari*, published in Latin in Verona in 1472 and in Italian in 1483 (Martindale 1979, p. 58). Hope 1985 takes Biondo to be the primary source, but see also Halliday 1994, who suggests that original texts, even in Greek, were consulted.
22. Plutarch, *Bioi paralleloi, Aimilios Paulos*, XXXII–XXXIV; Appian, *Romaica*, book VIII, Punic Wars, ch. IX, para. 66.
23. These are fully discussed in Martindale 1979, both in ch. 5 and in his individual catalogue entries. The Arch of Trajan at Benevento has a long frieze of a triumphal procession that Mantegna must have known from drawings; it should be noted that his son Ludovico studied the antiquities at Benevento in 1496 while in the entourage of Francesco Gonzaga II during the expedition to the Kingdom of Naples; Luzio and Torelli 1920–2, II, p. 160, cited by Lightbown 1986, p. 245 and Signorini 1996, p. 104, n. 12; letter from Ludovico to Francesco 26 May 1496: 'my practice is to visit those ancient remains and I take great consolation from this.' For the evident importance to Mantegna of drawings after the antique by others, see Leoncini 1993.
24. See Martindale 1979, pp. 78–9. An early autograph drawing in the J. Paul Getty Museum, Los Angeles, for the left-hand panel of the San Zeno altarpiece, is similar in type and scale (19.5 [cropped] × 13.5 cm, for a panel 212 × 125 cm) and has indications of pilasters and bases; see Verona 2006–7, pp. 195–9 and 201–3.
25. All this is discussed in Martindale 1979, ch. 6, and for the individual examples see entries by D. Ekserdjian in London and New York 1992.
26. Infrared reflectography was carried out on Canvases 4, 5 and 6 in 2006. I am grateful to Lucy Whitaker and Rupert Featherstone for giving me access to these images in 2008. In Canvas 4, there are minor

pentiments in the right arm, neck and shoulder of the blond youth and in the lines of the trumpet shafts. In Canvas 5 the most obvious change, also visible with the naked eye, is to the foot of the boy riding the elephant at the right.

27. The *Triumphs* are painted on closely woven linen twill canvases (Martindale 1979, p. 126, and see his fig. 275 for a macrophotograph). The medium has been variously identified. Fry thought that Mantegna probably painted in egg tempera and that Laguerre's repaints were in glue-size. In 1930 L.A. Jordan, a chemist at the Paint Research Station, came to similar, though provisional, conclusions (both reports in Royal Collection files). In 1974 it was tentatively concluded at the National Gallery, London, by John Mills (also drawing on analysis of samples and a report made by Joyce Plesters in 1962) that, while Laguerre's repaints were in oil, Mantegna's medium was egg tempera, but the possibility that glue size might have been the original medium seems not to have been investigated on that occasion (the reports are in the archives of the Scientific Department at the National Gallery), and might in any case have resisted the then available technology. In his survey of Mantegna's tempera technique, Rothe 1992, p. 84 (thanking John Brealey for paint samples), concluded: 'The binding medium seems to be animal glue.'
28. See Lightbown 1986, ch. IX, pp. 154–76, 'Mantegna in Rome'. The paintings were destroyed in the eighteenth century.
29. Kristeller 1902, doc. 123. Kristeller believed that the *Triumphs* were completed by 1494, as have many later writers, including Martindale 1979 and Lightbown 1986, p. 149. But there is no proof of completion to be found in Isabella d'Este's letter describing the visit of the 'Magnifico Giovanni de' Medici' to the *Triumphs*, probably then in the Castello di San Giorgio.
30. Martindale 1979, ch. 6, pp. 75–91. Interestingly, however, he proposed that this somewhat incoherent triplet of scenes might have been planned very early on; see Elam, 'Mantegna and Mantua', in London 1981, pp. 15–26, esp. 21–2, and Hope 1985.
31. Stated, with much the same supporting argument, in Hope 1985, Hope in London and New York 1992 and Hope in Mantua 2006b. In support of this later chronology, as Hope points out, is the documented deployment of only six canvases, described as 'the six paintings of the triumph of Caesar by the hand of the singular Mantegna' in a theatrical event of 1501, along a wall which could have accommodated two more; see Kristeller 1902, doc. 156. The apparently lost letter describing the scene is reproduced in Luzio and Paribeni 1940, pp. 10–15.
32. For the *Cybele* (NG902), Lightbown 1986, pp. 451–2.
33. Martindale 1979, p. 184, for the letter of 17 April 1506 from Venice describing the state of work on six carved and gilded 'coloni che vano ai telari di messer Andrea'; for the possible identification of these pilasters see Agosti 1992.
34. See note 22 above.
35. Jones 1988.
36. Signorini 1996; for the significance of the discovery, see also Landau 1997. The entries read (Signorini pp. 111–12): 'uno stampo de uno triumpho de rame, *ut supra*, mezzo taliato ... uno stampo de' Triumphi *ut supra*, taliato da ogni canto *ut supra*'. Suzanne Boorsch and David Landau had already concluded that some of the surviving early *Triumphs* prints come from plates engraved on both sides (London and New York 1992, p. 469) and cats 118, 120, 123, 126; Elam in Paris 2008–9, cats 162–4, 166).
37. For the Giovanni Antonio da Brescia (formerly known as Zoan Andrea) copies, see Boorsch in London and New York 1992, cats 117, 121, 127. See Agosti 2005, pp. 113–15, 119–20, for bibliography on the use of Mantegna's triumphal imagery at the Chateau de Gaillon; in the *Triumphs* woodcuts designed by Benedetto Bordon and cut in Venice by Jacopo of Strasbourg (comprehensively discussed in Massing 1990); and in the Holbeins' lost painted facade of 1517–19 for the house in Lucerne of Jakob von Hertenstein.
38. The National Gallery (NG1336) retains an old attribution to Liberale da Verona (around 1445–around 1526), but see Vinco 2018, pp. 364–5, cat. 120 for the suggestion that it is an early work by Liberale's pupil Niccolò Giolfino (around 1476–1555). The architecture is particularly subtle.
39. The fullest account of the Prague copies (inv. O1103) is in Antwerp 2004, cat. 51. For the many painted copies made of the *Triumphs* in the early seventeenth century, see Martindale 1979, ch. 9 and more recently, with examples that have come to light since, Arlt 2005.
40. For Rubens's procedures in the National Gallery picture (NG278), in which the canvases are stuck down on panel, see Balis in Tokyo 1994, p. 106 and Wood 2002, pp. 38–9, summarised in Agosti 2005, pp. 445–7.
41. Goethe 1898, 1. Abt., Band 49, pp. 266 ff.; translated in Gage 1980, pp. 160–5.
42. Ibid.
43. Ibid.
44. Campbell 2004b, p. 96, points out the connection between the phrase 'INVIDIA / SPRETA SVPERATA' in Canvas 2 and Mantegna's obsession with the opposition of envy to virtue as expressed in his *Virtus combusta* composition.
45. Fry 1902, p. 148.
46. These details are not discussed in the literature. The relatively modern shape of the scissors might suggest that they are later additions inserted by a restorer.

BIBLIOGRAPHY

The most comprehensive monographs on Andrea Mantegna in English remain Kristeller 1901 and Lightbown 1986. The exhibition catalogues Paris 2008–9, London and Berlin 2018–19, and Turin 2019 bring together a vast bibliography on the artist and include an overall assessment of the artist's production.

Agosti 1992
G. Agosti, *Le Nozze di Perseo*, Quaderni del Restauro, 8, Milan 1992

Agosti 2005
G. Agosti, *Su Mantegna I. La Storia dell'arte libera la testa*, Milan 2005

Alberti 2004
L.B. Alberti, *On Painting*, London 2004

Ames-Lewis 1993
F. Ames-Lewis (ed.), *Mantegna and 15th-Century Court Culture*, London 1993

Ames-Lewis 2000
F. Ames-Lewis, *The Intellectual Life of the Early Renaissance Artist*, New Haven and London 2000

Antwerp 2004
K.L. Belkin and F. Healey (eds), *A House of Art: Rubens as Collector*, exh. cat., Rubenshuis, Antwerp 2004

Arlt 2005
T. Arlt, *Mantegna 'Triumph Caesaris': Ein Meisterwerk der Renaissance in neuem Licht*, Vienna 2005

Armstrong 2008
L. Armstrong, 'Triumphal Processions in Italian Renaissance Book Illumination and Further Sources for Mantegna's Triumphs of Caesar', *Manuscripta*, 52, no. 1 (2008), pp. 1–63

Beard 2007
M. Beard, *The Roman Triumph*, Cambridge, MA and London 2007

Berzaghi 1990
R. Berzaghi, 'Francesco II e Vincenzo Gonzaga. Il Palazzo di San Sebastiano e il Palazzo Ducale', *Paragone*, 41, no. 485 (1990), pp. 62–73

Blumenröder 2008
S. Blumenröder, *Andrea Mantegna – the Grisailles: Painting, History and Ancient Art in the Paragone of the Quattrocento*, Berlin 2008

Bober and Rubinstein 1986
P.P. Bober and R. Rubinstein, *Renaissance Artists & Antique Sculpture: A Handbook of Sources*, London and Oxford 1986

Bourne 2008
M. Bourne, *Francesco II Gonzaga: The Soldier-Prince as Patron*, Rome 2008

Brown 1997
C.M. Brown, 'The Palazzo di San Sebastiano (1506–1512) and the Art Patronage of Francesco Gonzaga, Fourth Marquis of Mantua', *Gazette des Beaux-Arts*, 6, no. 129 (1997), pp. 131–80

Brown 2002
C.M. Brown, *Per dare qualche splendore a la gloriosa cità di Mantua: Documents for the Antiquarian Collection of Isabella d'Este*, Rome 2002

Brown and Delmarcel 1996
C.M. Brown and G. Delmarcel, *Tapestries for the Courts of Federico II, Ercole, and Ferrante Gonzaga, 1522–63*, Seattle and London 1996

Burchard and d'Hulst 1963
L. Burchard and R.A. d'Hulst, *Rubens Drawings*, 2 vols, Brussels 1963

Calvano 2010
T. Calvano et al. (eds), *Mantegna a Roma. L'artista davanti all'antico*, Rome 2010

Campbell 2004a
S.J. Campbell, *The Cabinet of Eros: Renaissance Mythological Painting and the Studiolo of Isabella d'Este*, New Haven and London 2004

Campbell 2004b
S.J. Campbell (ed.), *Artists at Court: Image-Making and Identity 1300–1550*, Chicago 2004

Campbell 2020
S.J. Campbell, *Andrea Mantegna: Humanist Aesthetics, Faith and the Force of Images*, London 2020

Canova 2001
A. Canova, 'Gian Marco Cavalli incisore per Andrea Mantegna e altre notizie sull'oreficeria e la tipografia a Mantova nel XV secolo', *Italia medioevale e umanistica*, 42 (2001), pp. 149–79

Canova 2007
A. Canova, 'L'inamoramento de Orlando da Mantova a Urbino (con una postilla mantegnesca)', *Lettere italiane*, 59, no. 2 (2007), pp. 226–35

Collins Baker 1934
C.H. Collins Baker, 'Mantegna Cartoons at Hampton Court II. The Preservation of the Cartoons', *The Burlington Magazine*, 64, no. 372 (1934), pp. 102–15

Di Monte 2007
M. Di Monte, 'Mantegna, Andrea', in *Dizionario biografico degli italiani*, no. 69, Rome 2007, pp. 181–94

Edinburgh 2002
J. Wood, *Rubens: Drawing on Italy*, exh. cat., National Galleries of Scotland, Edinburgh 2002

Ekserdjian 1997
D. Ekserdjian, *Correggio*, New Haven and London 1997

Elam 2019
C. Elam, *Roger Fry and Italian Art*, London 2019

Equicola 1521
M. Equicola, *Commentarii Mantuani*, n.p. 1521

Ferino-Pagden 2001
S. Ferino-Pagden, *Hochzeit Gonzaga. Die Brauttruhen der Paola Gonzaga und Andrea Mantegna*, Milan 2001 (from *FMR*, vol. 149)

Fry 1902
R. Fry, 'Andrea Mantegna', *Quarterly Review*, 195 (1902), pp. 139–58; reprinted in Elam 2019, pp. 324–35

Fusco and Corti 2006
L. Fusco and G. Corti, *Lorenzo de' Medici Collector and Antiquarian*, Cambridge 2006

Gage 1980
J. Gage, *Goethe on Art*, Berkeley, CA 1980

Goethe 1898
W. von Goethe, 'Triumphzug Von Mantegna', in *Werke*, vol. 1. Abt., Band 49, Weimar 1898, pp. 266 ff.

Halliday 1994
A.S. Halliday, 'The Literary Sources of Mantegna's Triumphs of Caesar', *Annali della Scuola Normale Superiore di Pisa*, vol. 3, 24, no. 1 (1994), pp. 337–96

Hope 1985
C. Hope, 'The Chronology of Mantegna's Triumphs', in A. Morrogh et al. (eds), *Renaissance Studies in Honor of Craig Hugh Smyth*, 2 vols, Florence 1985, pp. 297–309

Jones 1988
R. Jones, 'Mantegna and Materials', *I Tatti Studies. Essays in the Renaissance*, 2 (1988), pp. 71–90

Kristeller 1901
P. Kristeller, *Andrea Mantegna*, trans. S.A. Strong, London and New York 1901

Kristeller 1902
P. Kristeller, *Andrea Mantegna*, Berlin and Leipzig 1902

Landau 1997
D. Landau, 'Mantegna's Plates', *Print Quarterly*, 14 (1997), p. 81

Leoncini 1993
L. Leoncini, *Il Codice detto del Mantegna: Codice Destailleur OZ 111 della Kunstbibliothek di Berlino*, Rome 1993

Lightbown 1986
R.W. Lightbown, *Mantegna: With a Complete Catalogue of the Paintings, Drawings, and Prints*, Oxford 1986

London 1981
D. Chambers and J. Martineau (eds), *Splendours of the Gonzaga*, exh. cat., Victoria and Albert Museum, London 1981

London 2002
G. Bartrum, *Albrecht Dürer and his Legacy: The Graphic Work of a Renaissance Artist*, exh. cat., The British Museum, London 2002

London 2018
P. Rumberg and D. Shawe-Taylor (eds), *Charles I: King and Collector*, exh. cat., Royal Academy of Arts, London 2018

London and Berlin 2018–19
C. Campbell, D. Korbacher, N. Rowley, S. Vowles, *Mantegna & Bellini*, exh. cat., The National Gallery, London and Staatliche Museen zu Berlin, 2018–19, published London 2018

London and New York 1992
J. Martineau (ed.), *Andrea Mantegna*, exh cat., Royal Academy of Arts, London and Metropolitan Museum of Art, New York 1992, published Milan 1992

Luzio 1984
A. Luzio, *La Galleria dei Gonzaga venduta all'Inghilterra nel 1627–28: Documenti degli Archivi di Mantova e Londra raccolti ed illustrati da Alessandro Luzio*, Milan 1913, reprint Rome 1984

Luzio and Paribeni 1940
A. Luzio and R. Paribeni, *Il 'Trionfo di Cesare' di Andrea Mantegna*, Rome 1940

Luzio and Torelli 1920–2
A. Luzio and P. Torelli (eds), *L'Archivio Gonzaga di Mantova*, Verona, 1920–2

Mantua 2006a
F. Trevisani (ed.), *Andrea Mantegna e i Gonzaga: Rinascimento nel Castello di San Giorgio*, exh. cat., Castello di San Giorgio, Palazzo Ducale, Mantua 2006, published Milan 2006

Mantua 2006b
R. Signorini and D. Sogliani (eds), *A casa di Andrea Mantegna: Cultura artistica a Mantova nel Quattrocento*, exh. cat., Casa di Mantegna, Mantua 2006, published Milan 2006

Martindale 1979
A. Martindale, *The Triumphs of Caesar by Andrea Mantegna*, London 1979

Massing 1990
J-M. Massing, '"The Triumph of Caesar" by Benedetto Bordon and Jacobus Argentoratensis: Its Iconography and Influence', *Print Quarterly*, 7 (1990), pp. 9, 19–21

New York 2002
T.P. Campbell (ed.), *Tapestry in the Renaissance: Art and Magnificence*, exh. cat., The Metropolitan Museum of Art, New York 2002

Northampton, MA 1978
W. Stedman Sheard (ed.) *Antiquity in the Renaissance*, exh. cat., Smith Museum of Art, Northampton, MA 1978

Padua 1999
G.M. Canova et al. (eds), *La Miniatura a Padova dal medioevo al Settecento*, exh. cat., Palazzo della Ragione, Padua 1999

Paris 2008–9
G. Agosti and D. Thiébaut (eds), *Mantegna 1431–1506*, exh. cat., Musée du Louvre, Paris 2008–9

Pinelli 1985
A. Pinelli, 'Feste e trionfi: Continuità e metamorfosi di un tema', in *Memoria dell'antico nell'arte italiana*, vol. 2, Turin 1985, pp. 279–349

Rebecchini 2019
G. Rebecchini, 'Leonardo, Mantova e il ritratto di Isabella d'Este. Indagini su un'opera contesa', in F. Borgo, R. Maffeis and A. Nova (eds), *Leonardo e gli altri*, Venice 2019, pp. 175–96

Rebecchini 2021
G. Rebecchini, 'A Bronze Roundel for the Mantuan Court: Towards an Oeuvre of Gian Marco Cavalli', *The Burlington Magazine*, 163, no. 1422 (2021), pp. 798–805

Richards 2000
J. Richards, *Altichiero: An Artist and his Patrons in the Italian Trecento*, Cambridge 2000

Romano 1981
G. Romano, 'Towards the modern manner: from Mantegna to Raphael' in F. Hartt and D. Wilkins, *History of Italian Renaissance Art*, London 1981

Shaw 2019
C. Shaw, *Isabella d'Este: A Renaissance Princess*, London and New York 2019

Signorini 1996
R. Signorini, 'New Findings about Andrea Mantegna: His Son Ludovico's Post-Mortem Inventory (1510)', *Journal of the Warburg and Courtauld Institutes*, 59 (1996), pp. 103–18

Signorini 2010
R. Signorini et al. (eds), *Andrea Mantegna: Impronta del Genio*, 2 vols., Florence 2010

Stedman Sheard 1982
W. Stedman Sheard, 'Review of Martindale, *The Triumphs of Caesar*', *Renaissance Quarterly* 35, no. 1 (1982), pp. 79–82

Tavernor 1998
R. Tavernor, *On Alberti and the Art of Building*, New Haven and London 1998

Tokyo 1994
T. Nakamura (ed.), *Rubens and his Workshop: The Flight of Lot and his Family from Sodom*, exh. cat., Museum of Western Art, Tokyo 1994

Tosetti Grandi 2008
P. Tosetti Grandi, *I Trionfi di Cesare di Andrea Mantegna: Fonti umanistiche e cultura antiquaria alla corte dei Gonzaga*, Mantua 2008

Turin 2019
S. Bandera, H. Burns and V. Farinella (eds), *Andrea Mantegna. Rivivere l'antico costruire il moderno*, exh. cat., Palazzo Madama, Turin 2019, published Venice 2019

Vasari 1966–87
G. Vasari, *Le Vite de' più eccellenti pittori, scultori e architettori nelle redazioni del 1550 e 1568* [1568], 11 vols, R. Bettarini and P. Barocchi (eds), Florence 1966–87

Verona 2006–7
S. Marinelli and P. Marini (eds), *Mantegna e le arti a Verona 1450–1500*, exh. cat., Palazzo della Gran Guardia, Verona, 2006–7, published Venice 2006

Vinco 2018
M. Vinco, *Cassoni: Pittura profana del Rinascimento a Verona*, Milan 2018

Vowles 2019
S. Vowles, 'New Light on Mantegna's Triumphs of Caesar', *Master Drawings*, 57, no. 1 (2019), pp. 33–46

PICTURE CREDITS

Chantilly
Musée Condé, Chantilly © Grand Palais RMN (Domaine de Chantilly) / Michel Urtado: fig. 6, p. 36 (DE116).

Klagenfurt
Landesmuseum, Klagenfurt © akg-images / Erich Lessing: fig. 1, pp. 30–1.

London
© The National Gallery, London: fig. 1, p. 10; fig. 10, p. 21; fig. 11, p. 22; fig. 14, p. 26 left; fig. 15, p. 26 right; fig. 16, p. 27; fig. 11, p. 43; fig. 12, p. 44. The Royal Collection / His Majesty King Charles III © Royal Collection Enterprises Limited 2024 | Royal Collection Trust: cats 1–9.

Madrid
Museo Nacional del Prado, Madrid © Photographic Archive Museo Nacional del Prado: fig. 3, p. 12.

Mantua
Palazzo Ducale, Mantua © akg-images / MPortfolio / Electa: fig. 4, p. 14; © Ministero per i Beni e le Attività Culturali / Antonio Quattrone / Bridgeman Images: fig. 6, p. 16; © Scala / MBACT: fig. 5, p. 15.

Milan
Pinacoteca di Brera, Milan © Gabriele Croppi / Scala, Florence: fig. 8, p. 18.

New York
© The Metropolitan Museum of Art, New York: fig. 7, p. 17; fig. 10, p. 42 (2012.136.864); fig. 13, p. 45.

Paris
Musée du Louvre, Paris © Grand Palais RMN (Musée du Louvre) / Gérard Blot: fig. 13, p. 25; © Grand Palais RMN (Musée du Louvre) / Jean-Gilles Berizzi: fig. 9, p. 20; © Grand Palais RMN (Musée du Louvre) / Stéphane Maréchalle: fig. 12, p. 24; detail p. 8.
Musée du Louvre (Rothschild Collection), Paris © Grand Palais RMN (Musée du Louvre) / Thierry Le Mage: fig. 2, p. 32 (775 DR recto).

Private collection
Photo © Sotheby's / Bridgeman Images: fig. 3, p. 33.

Rome
© Roberto Piperno: fig. 4, p. 34.
© Photo Scala, Florence – courtesy of the Ministero per i Beni e le Attività Culturali e del Turismo: fig. 5, p. 35.

Verona
Church of San Zeno © Photo Scala, Florence: fig. 2, p. 11.

Vienna
© The Albertina Museum, Vienna: fig. 7, p. 37 (2585).

The Triumphs of Caesar

The Triumphs of Caesar: 1, The Trumpeters, about 1485–1506
Egg tempera on canvas, 270.3 × 281.2 cm
The Royal Collection / HM King Charles III

The Triumphs of Caesar: 2, The Triumphal Carts, about 1485–1506
Egg tempera on canvas, 271.2 × 281.1 cm
The Royal Collection / HM King Charles III

The Triumphs of Caesar: 3, The Trophy Bearers, about 1485–1506
Egg tempera on canvas, 270.5 × 281.2 cm
The Royal Collection / HM King Charles III

The Triumphs of Caesar: 4, The Vase Bearers, about 1485–1506
Egg tempera on canvas, 269.5 × 280 cm
The Royal Collection / HM King Charles III

The Triumphs of Caesar: 5, The Elephants, about 1485–1506
Egg tempera on canvas, 270 × 281.1 cm
The Royal Collection / HM King Charles III

The Triumphs of Caesar: 6, The Corselet Bearers, about 1485–1506
Egg tempera on canvas, 270 × 281.1 cm
The Royal Collection / HM King Charles III

The Triumphs of Caesar: 7, The Captives, about 1485–1506
Egg tempera on canvas, 270.5 × 280.2 cm
The Royal Collection / HM King Charles III

The Triumphs of Caesar: 8, The Musicians, about 1485–1506
Egg tempera on canvas, 270.2 × 280.5 cm
The Royal Collection / HM King Charles III

The Triumphs of Caesar: 9, Caesar on his Chariot, about 1485–1506
Egg tempera on canvas, 270.4 × 280.7 cm
The Royal Collection / HM King Charles III

Triumphs 1–6 are on loan to the National Gallery from its Bicentenary year in 2024.